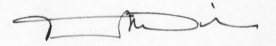

ART AS UNDERSTANDING

ART AS UNDERSTANDING

A Painter's Account of the Last Revolution in Art
and its Bearing on Human Existence as a Whole

by

FRANK AVRAY WILSON

Routledge & Kegan Paul

LONDON

First published *1963*
by Routledge & Kegan Paul Ltd.
Broadway House, *68–74* Carter Lane
London, E.C.*4*

Printed in Great Britain
by W. & J. Mackay & Co. Ltd.
Chatham, Kent

FOREWORD

BY HERBERT READ

THE function of a foreword is to say briefly a few things about a book which the author cannot with modesty say himself. Mr. Wilson is that very rare phenomenon—a painter who reflects on the significance of his activity and who is therefore driven to equip himself with a knowledge of the best that has been thought and said on the subject of life itself, its meaning and purpose. He does not do this in order to give additional significance to his own painting: art, as he makes perfectly clear, is not a metaphysical but a sensuous activity. But all our human faculties contribute in due degree to an existential unity, to our being and becoming, and it is Mr. Wilson's belief, a belief I fully share, that the function of art in this process is vital. The aesthetic activity is an essential feature of our biological evolution, an activity to which we owe the gradual emergence and refinement of our distinctively human consciousness. Should we deny or repress this faculty, we should lose our means of reacting creatively to our material environment and inevitably decline in intelligence and adaptability.

That is the general thesis, but there is a particular application of it to our present social predicament, which is a condition of estrangement from nature (usually called alienation) brought about by the progress of technology. Mr. Wilson sees art not only as 'the ceaseless adventure of being and becoming', but as a substitute for nature in a 'man-made and synthetic culture'. This is perhaps a point of view that is open to misinterpretation: art is a part of nature rather than a substitute for it, and even if we interpret nature to include our human nature, there is still a sense in which we are dependent on a direct contact with organic processes, from which we derive not only our material sustenance, but also receive a spiritual resonance. It is true that art has a function specific to our industrial society, and that the artist can impart a human quality to the products of that society. But he does this in virtue of a sensibility that is open to the whole visible (and invisible) world.

Those who are worried by the evident conflict between art and science in our time will find in Mr. Wilson an artist fully equipped to discuss this problem. His knowledge of modern science and philosophy is matched, not only by his knowledge of art history and aesthetics, but also by a creative approach that is prepared to find a practical synthesis. Mr. Wilson knows, from his own experience as a painter, that the artist can advance into new areas of consciousness, can invent new symbols and by their means reach a deeper understanding of reality. Art, he would affirm, is engaged on the same research as science, and to the élite who are prepared to follow him (and one of his claims is that the understanding of art demands the exercise of faculties at least as fine as any involved in physics or astronomy) the artist can communicate the inner reality of man, to correspond to the scientist's revelation of the inner reality of the physical order.

This is not Mr. Wilson's first book. He published a more technical analysis of the creative process five years ago (*Art into Life*). These two volumes are complementary and together constitute a comprehensive and profound analysis of the social significance of the art of our time.

HERBERT READ

CONTENTS

vii

ILLUSTRATIONS

(*Between pages 38 and 39*)

Reproductions of a selection of the main
kinds of paintings described in the text are
given at the end of the book.

I

ART AS A NECESSARY ACTIVITY

THIS is an attempt to put into words a painter's conclusions on the bearing of art and existence. It is a fact that an artist's attitudes to his art affect his outlook on every other matter. A person who claims that his views on education, on the nuclear deterrent, on love, have nothing to do with his art, is not an artist.

Such a conditioning might be thought to concern the artist alone, and have no bearing on others' problems. To this the artist replies that art is the most profoundly human of all activities, and that a view of existence guided by art is the most genuinely humanizing. It is the aim of this book to show that the artist's attitude to things, springing from his art, has something to offer others in an age of considerable confusion, and in the course of it to emphasize the importance of art in the world today.

The emotional basis of art

Since art can mean an almost endless variety of things, it is necessary to begin by saying what it is to mean in this book.

The Age of Reason necessarily encouraged a reasonable view of art. From the Renaissance to the close of the nineteenth century art tried to go the way of science, in serving more and more the world of appearances. If art gained in immediacy and popularity, it lost in the intangible extensions which other cultures have considered its most essential ingredient. A thorough reliance on reason can only end in relegating art and artists to an inferior category, as did Plato in his ideal rational republic. The triumph of scientific materialism in the nineteenth century left only room for an etiolated, realistic art. Artists requiring a greater freedom of expression could but tear themselves from a society so dictated by reason.

But the science on which this reasonable art was founded has gone. Such particles of matter as electrons, once believed to be

firm material bits, have been found to defy a strict material definition, and psychology has discovered a mental order very different
from the common day.

This broadening of outlook allows such an elusive and previously suspicious thing as human emotionalism to be looked at
more seriously. If this emotional aura is so discreet in the common
occurrences of daily living as to be ignorable, it is blatantly evident
in the heights of existence, in the desperate longings and thrills of
life and of love, in the climaxes and crises of existence, as it always
is in art. So-called aesthetic emotion becomes an accentuation of a
condition chronic to all human beings.[1]

Being the counters of practical communication, words are not
ideally suited for describing this emotionalism. But if one cannot
define emotionalism accurately, it is none the less a fact. A reasonable view of life has been needed to take care of food, shelter and
survival, but the earliest human beings also required companion-
ship and love, and felt fear and joy, awe and gratitude, sorrow and
elation, all of which required emotional routes of communication
in facial expression, in gesture, in the accented phrase, in the cry
and the shout and the trembling breath.

It would seem that such an emotional interchange between
human beings came even before words, the only possible way of
explaining the poet's ability to revive an emotionalized message
out of them to this day. Only a narrow-minded reliance on reason
since the Renaissance has allowed this primordial fact to be
hidden—that human beings are human not through reason but
because they are emotionalized animals, and that the faculty of
reason, instead of being primary and exclusive, is on the contrary
secondary and derivative.

A reasonable art is not fully art, any more than pain can be
accounted for as a purely nervous activity. But it does remain
necessary to see how such an apparently strange thing as emotionalism came into being in the order of natural things. In
accounting for it, one will automatically find the best of all justi-
fications for the existence and function of art in human life.

The origins of human emotionalism

Many birds are highly emotionalized, and their elaborate displays
and colourings are emotionalizing devices.[2] Among mammals,

there is plenty of evidence of it. Although usually connected with breeding and sex, emotionalism in animals tends naturally to overflow into expressive and playful channels which tend to become ends and pursuits in themselves. A rudimentary aesthetic faculty exists in some birds, notably the bower-birds, and in monkeys and apes quite a remarkable capacity exists for making aesthetically acceptable imageries.[3]

A sex connexion in human emotionalism can be found readily enough, in the intense emotionalisms of puberty, in the control of the voice by the sex hormones. Whereas sex in almost all animals is straightforward copulation, fun and run, the human brain, which has depended on learning for its development, a process still repeated in every growing individual, can but mature slowly so as to give as much time as possible for each generation to profit from experience. So the human infant required prolonged parental care from the very beginnings of the human story, a care that could only be properly provided by a close co-operation of the mates.

Co-operation must entail control of the universal, self-satisfying opportunism of a purely physical coitus, and only a mechanism that could override the primitive call to immediate gratification could have a chance of success. So it was that from the very beginnings of human creation emotionalism was selected as a force which could challenge and supersede the physiological by diametrically opposed appeals and gratifications. Emotionalism is indeed basic and not only made possible the evolution of the brain but prepared the way for reason in its time to appear. Reason can only function humanly if due attention is paid to human emotional needs, a fact that we have tended to forget since the Age of Reason. It is an emotionalized sexuality rather than a physical opportunism that can account for the most truly human traits.[4]

A necessary feature of this sex emotionalism is that it should be idealizing, enabling immediate satisfactions to be surmounted and transcended, as well as encouraging a harmonious and selfless procreative co-operation. The ready sacrifices of love, the aspirations for the beautiful, the harmonious, the noble, the pure, are human traits that have been genetically enforced by selective evolution, for only thereby could the human brain have emerged from a more purely animal antecedent.

To enforce these promptings to behaviour compatible with human survival and evolution the human face and the human body, as well as certain aspects of nature, were selectively chosen to be seen as beautiful, a choice that in time became instinctive and embedded in the human mind. And so it is that these were the very first 'works of art', a natural and genetic aesthetics which was essential to human survival.

The human voice, the springboard of all subsequent music, plays an obvious role as an emotional stimulant, apparently the oldest, for its emotionalizing mechanisms are the most perfected. The aspiration of all the arts to music, as much as the insistence of the academicians on the primary importance of the human form in art teaching, thus finds biological support.

Just as the innate musicality of the human voice evolved into music—the most primitive people have theirs—so the innate aesthetics of an emotionalized view of nature led on to the visual arts. The quite remarkable emotionalizing sensitivity of the eyes is often overlooked by the clamour of its practical functions. Yet the eyes have been evolved and finely perfected for much more than to see things clearly. No purely practical reasons can account for the quite exceptional sensitivity of the human eye to colour, and the sensitivities of the eye and mind to the harmonies of line and form exceed any purely practical intention. So perfected are the eye and ear as emotional conduits that one can agree with Lévy-Bruhl that the emotionalized view of things preceded the critical, analytical ability to see things as separate material objects. The most primitive and primordial view of the world was a thoroughly emotionalized one.

But this emotionalism was perforce discreet; it could not be allowed to interfere with the practical obligations of daily living, and so this aesthetic function, although highly perfected and powerful, was made to be intuitive, spontaneous, and unanalytical, operating mostly unawares, in what psychologists have come to call the unconscious.

To understand how art has evolved from a nature-connected aesthetics, it is necessary to emphasize that all the aesthetic criteria are in truth projections from the human mind upon appropriate objects and scenes, a projection which is, of course, not realized; we assume blithely that colour is 'in' the flower, that the harmony of a shape belongs to the shape, whereas these are basically emotionalized attributes bequeathed to external things.

This is an important conclusion, for it follows that *any* object is, theoretically, capable of receiving this projection. Nature as such is only a convenience. And although natural shapes and objects may be the most ready and convenient receptacles for this aesthetic display, any object, whether made by man, machine, or by hazard, can be found suitable for it, and the story of world art is a dramatic confirmation of the tireless quest for substitutes to nature's stage. Art acquires its full human stature as the primitive dependence on nature is weaned and metamorphosed, in the song-borrowing instrument, in the substituting daub of pigment.

In other words, art naturally tends to go abstract, but the convenience of nature ensures that usually some sort of tie with the visible world is retained. But this should not obscure the fact that art always, even when most figurative, reflects an emotionalized order which is quite distinct and different in origin and intention from the physical appearances of things. Its most ancient intention was to de-physicalize the human view, to make human beings see things, however subtly, differently, and so art has always been the evidence of an 'other' order in the midst of man.

Reason tends to dismiss as unreal and insignificant anything different from it and from the visible world that it has been evolved to serve. So it is that realism, the art of reason, is so opposed to the abstract. Realism is, of course, possible, but it can never be quite free from some measure of this otherness if it is to be art at all. And realism is not the most natural, straightforward art, as we tend to think. In truth, it is the most unnatural, requiring a large repertory of techniques and deceptive devices, the art evolved to suit an age which had placed all its trust in reason. Any correction of this is bound to restore the inbuilt tendency of all art to be in some way abstract, and, in certain circumstances, to move openly towards greater degrees of abstraction.

The duality in art

The aesthetic emotions which have arisen in association with nature—feelings for beauty and the harmonies of form, line and colour—do not account for the full play of emotionalism one encounters in art. There is an opposite gamut of more primitive emotion in the excitements, in the awe and anguish, in the tensions and throbs of world art. One can well imagine that if animals have no feeling for beauty, they know too well the meaning of fear, of excitement and anguish, of longing and satisfaction. Since the mark of man is the passage from the animal to the emotionalized human being, one sees that the nature-connected emotions one finds in art are in truth the 'humanizing emotions',[5] stimulating the essential motivations to acting humanly, whereas the more primitive gamut must represent animal relics still lurking and smouldering in the psyche. One can also assume that it has been the intention of selective evolution to balance these potentially dangerous antihuman reminders by the humanizing emotions, and this is just what one finds under the more normal conditions of existence, when human beings can, in fact, manage to be human. When dehumanizing agencies of one kind or another come into force, in nature's own hostilities, in the complications and frustrations of culture and civilization, then the somnolent subhuman motivations become aroused and man becomes in various ways no longer properly human.[6]

This accounts for an opposition between what can be termed the 'existential' and the 'humanizing',[7] an opposition that is active in all art, and accounts for a good deal of its satisfactions and thrills, for the conditions of life are very rarely entirely compatible with human expression developing freely. The more man has progressed in terms of culture and civilization, visibly the more he has paid the price in threats of antihumanism, and as a parallel art has also increased as a corrective and as a human reminder and reinstatement. The different forms that art takes in the endless variations of living in different times and places can be attributed to the varying ways in which this fundamental opposition is reconciled. This reconciliation is the key to an understanding of the human condition, for the human being, it has been noted, is by nature an emotionalized animal, with motivations quite different from the entire animal pre-establishment; the dualism, the clash of animal precedent and emerging humanization, is an essential part of the human drama, and without this tension and struggle there is no human progress, and every art worthy of the name takes due notice of this ceaseless dialectic in the web of living.[8]

Art in place and time

This dialectic gives to art an endless possibility of metamorphosis, of change and alteration in response to the changes of human reaction to life. But since art belongs to a quite different order from the material changes of existence, one cannot expect a simple and predictable response of art to life. Response there is, but it is unpredictable in kind and extent, a response sufficiently certain none the less to serve as a reliable anthropological and sociological reference.

The oldest human art probably consisted of floral gatherings, found-objects and skin markings.[9] Flowers are the most powerful emotionalizing agencies provided by nature, and one can but presume that the human species was created in an environment in which flowers abounded, for in no other way could the remarkable human colour-sense have evolved: functions do not simply come into being; they have to be exercised and developed with reference to an external necessity. In some way, all colourful objects made and used by human beings are flower-substitutes. Floral arrangements, from the simplest gatherings of the child to the elaborate structures still made from flowers in many parts of the world, are the first man-made art objects. But beads and trinkets and jewellery, body-markings and later weavings can still be looked upon as flower-substitutes.

Flowers are also innately abstractable and lend themselves readily to quite abstract arrangements. In this sense the use of paint simulates a primordial use of flowers for emotional expression, of flower arrangements and the juices of flowers and plants for body and bark markings. It can also be imagined that when the human voice was being evolved and still precariously established those earliest human beings must have been drawn to the song of birds, nature's already proficient musicians; man's emotional attachment to such things as flowers and birds runs deep.

The use of colours, even in quite abstract ways, echoes man's original floral affinites, and so is 'naturalistic' in feeling, tending to evoke what have been called the humanizing emotions. Such a naturalistic art prevails when nature is sufficiently kind and generous to allow human beings to be human. Although this has not usually been the case—for hundreds of thousands of years mankind was subjected to devastating and dehumanizing ice ages—there are grounds for thinking that human creation took place under such ideal conditions, in preglacial times or in one of the long interglacial periods.

When nature becomes somewhat less bountiful the first human

reaction is to enhance the aesthetic appeals of nature in works of art; the necklace of coloured things, the body markings, do just this. In our own civilization Abstract Impressionism has been a last desperate attempt to smuggle nature in. When conditions of life become more harassing, then the more primitive aspects of the psyche become aroused and demand expression and outlet.

Left to themselves, the aroused intrusions from the primitive aspects of mind would easily run to the anti-human, the diabolical and the demented—they do that often enough in the course of history—but it is the business of the humanizing mechanisms to parry this threat, to redeem and reclaim the intrusion, a function evident in the bestiaries and devilries of world art. In various ways, these strange underworld objects are beautified, coloured, given more harmonious form. They can also be given a characteristically human feature, order, which can range from a discreet rearrangement of the visible to increasing geometric disciplines which can end in quite abstract and entirely geometric imageries. The gist of this device is to control the primitively organic thrusts, to impose an order essentially human upon them.

Although the humanizing emotions originally were evolved in close association with visible nature, with organic things, the organic is also the bridgehead to all that has preceded man, to the remotest and most primitive animalizing vestiges always lurking in the depths of the psyche, ready to spring back into the bulbous, the proliferative, and the obscene. So it is that a rigid purifying order becomes the embodiment of the most humanizing opposition to the hazards of the organic. The geometric extreme usually appears only in thoroughly denatured or extremely harassing conditions of life, as in deserts or jungles.[10] Often enough one finds both a freely naturalistic and a geometric art in the same community, and it is evident that some people naturally prefer the one to the other. The important point to bear in mind is that both the freely naturalistic and the geometric have their genesis in an association with nature, with the external visible world, and amount to the human attempts to retain, enhance, or redeem it.

But when conditions become so harassing that nature appears antihuman and fearful, ominous and cruel, then a totally different aesthetic mechanism comes into play. Here art rejects nature altogether: this is Expressionism. Since the commonest human lot has been one of cruel persecution by nature, not only in many

8

parts of the world today but especially in the dehumanizing trials of the ice ages, Expressionism is by far the most frequent human art.

Art as emotional adaptation

If the fundamental difference between man, as an emotional animal, and the external order is borne in mind, the imperative need for emotional adaptation will be realized. Man does not simply live in the physical world. He must find emotionalized meaning in it, else the physical order amounts to a denial of his fundamental humanity. This is not a problem when nature is entirely kind and congenial; then man can live a blissful, perfectly natural and largely unconscious existence. But any change from this, and an emotional adaptive response becomes essential, and this can take the two forms we have found, either an emphasis of naturalism in art, or a revolt against nature.

This emotionalized reconciliation has been so important to human evolution and survival that not only is the urge to art and the mechanism of it highly explicit, but within the mind itself, an elaborate and fully established 'inner world' has come into being as the seat of the specifically human order. Art operates on the surest and truest of human foundations, the inner reality of man, the one means of externalizing and exercising that reality.

Such a force has art and its inner establishment become that it assumes a new magnitude in human life. Far away in the mists of prehistory are its biological roots; no longer purely serving sex passively, it becomes an active leaven in human progress, a stimulus to new groping, to new views, restless, germinal.[11] It becomes the means of social realization, the outward exercise of the inner spirit of social man.[12] And since physical human evolution has to all appearances come to an end, it is the means of extension and continued progress and evolution in a quite new realm without the impediments and barriers of the physical order.[13]

Art is thus at the very heart of the human problem. The question what is art inevitably passes over into the trembling question what is man. And the perennial 'otherness' of art and its ceaseless, dynamic manifold in time and place should teach us that to expect a definite and final answer to that question is erroneous. Art bears visible evidence to the profound unseizability and nonfinality of man, to the ceaseless adventure of being and becoming.

The importance of art today is accentuated by the collapse of the most ancient of humanizing agencies, in nature itself, in religion, in the bonds of family and community loyalties. It is the most merciful and astounding fact that art, although evidently born of nature and fortified by nature, can come in time to take on the emotionalizing and humanizing role of a forsaken and dismissed nature, in the midst of a man-made and synthetic culture. More than any other, this consideration emphasizes the supreme importance of art in modern industrial society, and makes the function and service of art today singular and different.[14] Art is no longer merely emotional communication and exercise; it has become the one means of converting the new, synthetic environment into an overall work of art which alone will be able to replace nature as a humanizing agency. The survival of man may well depend on the success or failure of this substitution.

But what has been said only applies to an art which is intimately related to the actual human condition. Arts which have come into being to serve other and different conditions, no matter how enjoyable they may still happen to be, have no bearing on the human predicament, and we shall now proceed as best we may to an examination of this kind of vital, valid art in the form of painting, related to the greatest human crisis.

2

ART IN A PERIOD OF CHANGE

The sources of European art

EUROPEAN civilization has been fed by two different springs, the one matter-of-fact, business-like, materialistic, coming from the great Mediterranean and Middle Eastern civilizations of antiquity, the other tenebrous and unworldly, coming both from the twilights of the pagan North and from the esoteric East. The Greeks and Romans had gone a long way along the road of reason; their art had come to avoid ambiguity, was realistic and precise. In the calamities of the dark ages, this trend was temporarily reversed, but after the first millenium A.D., a time of strange internal upheaval and far fusions,[15] a growing feeling for order, explicit in Gothic, returns, and the Expressionism of Romanesque, the mysteries of Byzantium slowly give way to realism and calculation. In the south of Europe, a reasonable view of life returned.

The Renaissance and a return of realism

The mysterious and the elusive are out of place in the sunlit lands of Italy, but the main reason for a return of the practical view of life there came with a revival of trade and commerce which had been so disrupted in the cataclysms of the dark ages. The rise of trading cities such as Venice, Genoa, and Florence brought increasing wealth as well as a growing control over nature for human ends and needs. Nature could afford to be seen as pleasant and benign, and realism and naturalism in art returned with the triumph of the practical view of life. The Renaissance ideology depended for its successes in life as in art on an implicit faith in the order and infallibility of the material realm. Science itself could only develop in the confidence of such a faith. In line with a general cultural preoccupation with the palpable, the weighable and the seeable, art became preoccupied with the analysis of vision and with the elaboration of techniques able to evoke reality-sensations.

In Renaissance painting from Giotto and Duccio onwards objects are solid entities immersed in a neutral, Newtonian space, and the individuality of things is always respected, even when mistings and apparent blurrings are resorted to. Indeed, as Professor Gombrich remarks, Leonardo achieved his most remarkable feats of lifelikeness by blurring just those which are most obviously lifelike and so forcing us to notice them. This is just the opposite of an attempt to render ambiguously. Drawing becomes the supreme means of material delimination and emphasis, and the world-view of an entire age is shown in the emphasis placed on its importance. In painting, the step-by-step build-up, the juxtapositions of paint, the enhancement of natural structure and texture by brushwork, induce a strong feeling of externality.

Naturalism and Impressionism

While many artists tried to vie with science in an accurate representation of nature, the more sensitive realists always retained a discreet lyrical touch, a freedom of application which, while respecting obvious appearances, none the less subtly overrides it. At its best, drawing was verveful, and in painting pigment can be seen to run with a discreet freedom of the shapes, the scumbles can be seen to trespass the accurate requirements of surface.

This remarkable quality of the best of European painting was to enable it to move towards abstraction with Impressionism,[16] for evidently the strokes, scumbles, and blobs of paint, the runs of line and brush, are not a part of reality; they are quite abstract in themselves, and it is only the manner in which they are used that conjures up feelings of realness, of nature-related sensations.

The reason that this is possible, that quite abstract, symbolic touches can evoke feelings of nature and external reality, comes from the fact that reality for human beings is always basically an emotionalized interpretation of it, never entirely physical. It is not so much the actual shapes of things that matter humanly, but an overall emotionalized reinterpretation of them. It will be recalled that emotionalism, from its sexual origins, is basically different from the physical and the physiological. So any apparent fit between the physical appearance of things and its emotional interpretation is illusional: the difference remains fundamental and never entirely mendable. This being so, the emotionally flavoured view of all things is never direct, but is always to some degree symbolic. We may assume that what we see is as it is, yet in subtle ways an emotionalized transformation of actual physical reality occurs.

It is this transformed and more highly emotionalized view of things that the artist manages to catch, and so it is that he can heighten one's reality-feelings while yet taking flagrant liberties with reality. Without fully realizing it, our most casual view of nature echoes the kind of emotional abstraction that the artist performs on canvas, in the sweep of hills, in the filligree of branches, in the architecture of trees and the granularities of stones, in the runs of sand and the softnesses of dunes, in the swaying of grass fields and the tremblings of leaves, the ripples of water and the sparkles of light, and in the profundities of shadows where one can imagine an infinity of happenings, all pregnantly abstract and usable in a rich symbolism. It is these and other qualities that the artist uses intuitively, in the transcribed sweeps of pigment, the runs of line and the impastos of paint, in trembling touches of colour, in mistings and glazings and sfumatos. It is no coincidence that Impressionism was achieved through colour essentially, for colour is the freest of all potential symbols, usable anywhere, everywhere.

Since symbolic transcription is the only way that the utterly different emotional order can be given visible, embodied expression, and since it is this emotional glimmer in all things that gives us our poignant sense of realness and meaning in them, the artist can truly say that in wielding a symbolic language he renders a greater sensation of reality.

This symbolic rendering can only be done intuitively: referring to an order utterly different from external reality and the reason that goes with it, the symbol is not findable and usable by any reasonable, analytical means. So it is that the artist only manages to pull off this symbolic transcription when he is moved, when intuition can take over. This essential elusiveness and imprecisability of the symbolic function of art is important, for it is a human trait, promoted by reason, to try to pin things down and pull them apart in isolation. If this is done, the symbol immediately ceases to be, and it is even somewhat misleading to talk of one particular symbol, as some sort of isolated, fabricated thing—the work of art is always a whole, an orchestration of symbolic ingredients which cannot be separated out, and it is this that makes art a totally different function from reasonable knowing.

Abstract Impressionism

The shapes of recognizable things have obvious symbolic powers on their own, but, as one can expect, their symbolic appeal is relatively superficial. Immensely important to the practical, daily life, they are none the less the least freely emotionalized. If art, in the Age of Reason, had to provide obviously recognizable things, there was always another kind of symbolic appeal in the 'matière' of the painting itself, in the reality-sensations which the juxtaposition of paint, the textural copies of the brush, the mimetic flow of external lines and structures, provided, and in colour which was always potentially free and extractable even when it was most closely associated with figuration. As the demand in painting for a close attention to the visible world diminished, so this innate tendency of painting to go abstract was realized. Many explanations of the move away from traditional realism have been suggested. Photography, it has been said, did away with the need for realism. But the real causes are probably deeper. The industrial revolution brought about a fundamental alteration of human existence, in a move away from nature, and since realism in art had been closely associated with nature, there was a reaction from within the emotionalized inner-world itself.

This took a variety of forms, but the most immediate and obvious one was an instinctive attempt by artists to enhance reality-sensations of nature in art. As nature is threatened, devastated, man reacts to retain, accentuate, and substitute her ancient appeals, on which the entire history of the humanizing emotions has depended for their evolution and exercise. The reaction was indeed from the depths. Abstract Impressionism is the most desperate attempt to retain these reality-feelings of nature in abstract paint, especially in colour, and all its technical achievements can be traced to traditional art. Much greater freedom was enjoyed, but the technical devices, the respect for the abilities of paint to transcribe naturalistic emotions, was retained and explored to the full. The painting is still a condensed, heightened 'piece of life', however scrambled it may be, no matter how apparently free it happens to be of recognizable objects. As in nature, colour is used 'musically', in subtleties of tone variation and orchestration, and colours are wielded together by just those sparkles of light, of white and greys that one finds in nature, pulling all its diversities of appeal into a harmonious whole.

Although highly camouflaged by the scramblings, space is still the same kind of space as in traditional painting, a space in which objects are immersed, a space which is itself neutral, a mere container, a space which enables separation and recession, even if it is only in the brush strokes. And as in all traditional art, time is static. As the painting is a 'piece of life', a condensed fragment from the world, so time within it is stopped. The passage of time in traditional art can only be rendered most artificially and inadequately, and movement can only be an illusion: the bird never flies, the wheels never turn. And as a result, experiential time is felt to be a 'hushed moment', a time removed and static. Now the Abstract Impressionist, although his dither and scramblings enable him to assume an apparent freedom and movement, does not break out of this kind of space and time. In paintings of Sam Francis, of Riopelle, apparently quite abstract, the strong flavour of nature remains, and the spaces and time are of the external order.

The seekers of order

What may be called the lyrical, impressionistic, naturalistic reaction was not the only one to the changes in human existence that began towards the end of the eighteenth century. As the disruption of the ancient ties of man and nature became more ruthless, so an equally ancient mechanism in the human mind—to impose an order upon the face of things—came into evidence.

In visible nature a sense of order and coherence is given by the mathematical relationships of things. In traditional art this spatial orchestration accounts for a good deal of its emotional appeal, the symbolization of an ordering and rearrangement specifically human. In the sketch-books of the great masters one finds much evidence of the natural tendency for this kind of symbolic order to go the way of mathematics, the round forms become bounded by planes, the frolics of line become contained by segments.

There can be no doubt that if shape and form are dispensed with, as in a quite abstract art, so one also removes the possibility of this symbolic order in things. To the traditional realist the weakening of figuration which came with progressive Impressionism must seem as an opening of the doors to potential chaos, and one does find a branch of Impressionism going that way, in a lush, flamboyant Fauvism, in gross exaggerations of extravagant colour.

The human mind is a reactive mechanism; and this event was met by a craving for order and restraint. This was not a contrived, calculated, artificial reaction. The emotionalization of sex, aimed at the control of primitive sex freedoms, would have had need for strong restraint, for control and emotional discipline, both within the mind and in the things seen of the world without. The seeking of ordered relationships—leading to mathematics itself ultimately—comes from this primordial need for visible reminders of an urgent human virtue, the control of the 'animal passions' in humanization. So it is that the evidences of organic extravagance and lushness in nature tend to sponsor a corrective reaction for order, not only a seeking of the order everywhere in nature itself, in the harmonies of colour, in the underlying structure of the landscape, in the architecture of trees and branches, but an actual projection of an order which is specifically human and entails a rearrangement of nature, which can best be done in art, and which can go all the way to a complete mathematical transcription of the visible world. It is there, discreetly assimilated and barely apparent in the great masters; it is more evident in Cézanne, blatantly so in Cubism, and finally in triumph in Constructivism and the recent revivals of 'hard edge'.

This is not something peculiar to our culture, although the gross dismissal of nature and the immense challenges of industrial and urban life appear to have called it into a very clear statement. One finds it in Negro art, and elsewhere. There are no doubt the more natural puritans, as well as the more natural libertines, and cultures are also variable in their free or more disciplined expressions, in periods of abandon or containment, the disciplines of the early Romans and Spartans contrasted with the dissolutions of late Rome and the orgies and dissipations of baroque. The favour of the lyrical or of the geometric in art does appear to be related to human attitudes, to the ways of life.

A preference for the geometric sensibility or for a freer symbolism in visible things is therefore variably human, and both have strong genetic, ingrained roots. Their variation is part of the human reaction to life and living. But while admitting this, one must also realize that with each goes an entire nucleation of reaction and feeling, which are fundamentally opposed and contrary. The geometric spirit is visibly compatible with order and calculation, the free with spontaneity, and if a geometric spirit prevails, then it must follow that certain things are foreign to it and cannot be understood by it. Pascal differentiated acutely between what he called 'l'esprit géometrique' and 'l'esprit de finesse', and points out that the former is useless for understanding the nature of life. There is, in fact, he rightly says, no single, definable 'nature' to man. 'Know then, haughty man, what a paradox you are to yourself. Humble yourself, impotent reason . . . learn that man infinitely surpasses man.' And this, from a mathematician, is a truly remarkable admission. In a sense that Pascal would have understood, we can say today that the geometric spirit is one of the most skilful and destructive manifestations of antihumanism.

None the less, it is a necessary function, and its dialectic with the free is a part of man's nature: it is not an artificial device, although it does tend to be evoked in artificializing cultures and conditions of life. The lyrical or impressionistic, and the geometric, belong to opposite poles of a naturalistic spectrum. The naturalism of Abstract Impression is obvious, but the superficially synthetic elaborations of Constructivism and 'hard edge' should not be allowed to deceive one. In origin, in emotion, and, above all, in technique, the entirely geometric image belongs to the traditional order,[17] evoking a thoroughly classical, Newtonian space, and shapes and objects within it are as thoroughly Euclidean.

Even the passage from the lyrical to the geometric is possible, as one sees in the evolution of Mondrian, and in the periodical changes in the life work of Kandinsky, proving the nature connexions of the geometric. Here is the clear evidence of the connexion of the geometric image with the traditional order which served nature, and the falsity of the claim, still being made by its revivalists, that the geometric is a synthetic, nature-free art.

17

A painter like Ben Nicholson has even visibly maintained the compromise between the two, and Pasmore's more recent work shows a naturalistic softening. The term synthetic cubism is a deception, and Constructivism and 'hard edge' are not synthetic achievements free of all nature.

The Traditional Modern

It might be thought that since the need for order is so great, then this genetically promoted tendency to find mathematical relations in things is excellent and justified. Without a doubt, it met ideally the classical and the traditional requirements in art.[18] But times have changed, and the emotional criteria of the Renaissance are no longer valid in an artificial, denatured age.

Fortunately, a Newtonian space is not the only kind of space which can be symbolized in art, nor is a precise Euclidean geometry the only geometry. One finds different expressions of this primordial need for order in the perspective of the Orient, and in the most recent painting, which are non-Euclidean.

Nor, indeed, are the scramblings of the Abstract Impressionists the only possible way of moving to a totally abstract lyrical imagery. Expressionism, long neglected in Europe, has lately opened up the way to a quite different kind of abstract image entirely free from natural influences. What has to be stressed repeatedly is that the kind of apparently total abstraction that one comes upon in Abstract Impressionism and in 'hard edge' are in manner and spirit entirely classical and traditional, emotionally and technically, that they were in a true sense implied in traditional art and technique, and were at some time inevitable, but that they do not make for the fundamentally and radically new; they are the last manipulation of the old imagery.

When 'modern' art is becoming more widely accepted, it is a pity to have to point this out, for the bulk of abstract paintings going about today will fall under this definition. But it is necessary, if we are to come to the really new paintings of our times, to realize this clearly, for the camouflaged naturalism of this kind of abstract art means that when a person has overcome his prejudice that a painting must have figurative, recognizable cues in it, then he discovers enormous attractions in this abstract painting. What seemed at first to be a denial of nature and of reality becomes an enhancement of it, and the pleasurable and comforting external world is retained. It is an observable fact that people who have come to accept this kind of painting and the rising batch of modern masters who supply it, not only enjoy it, but defend it ferociously against the newest paintings which visibly and, to them, offensively contradict the traditional painter-liness and good finish of the Traditional Abstract. To them, the new painting is apt to appear as the enemy, the nemesis of all art.

New age, new art

The relatedness of art and life means that in a welter of all kinds of unrelated art carried over from the past and from other cultural influences, one can be best fitted to pick out what really matters if one has some feeling in the first place of what is meant by contemporary existence. It is surprising how many people fail to realize the fundamental differences of life in the second half of the twentieth century from all that has gone before, even from life a generation ago.

Although human beings are physiologically and physically identical with their forebears, there are a whole array of emotional responses that are specific to the age. As an isolated entity, man does not exist. The specifying environment of modern man is undoubtedly the result of science, of technology, and of the industrial and urban revolutions that have come with them. It is to the impact of these quite new things on the emotional nature of human beings that we must now turn, in order to understand the premises of a radically new art, free of nature.

3

THE ROOTS OF REVOLUTION

Science and the industrial revolution

HUMAN beings have always wanted to have power over nature and use its forces and energies for their own ends. Often, these forces have seemed so complex, so negligent of human interest, and the human being has felt so helpless and overwhelmed, that he has handed over authority to powers supernatural and magical. Yet the earliest flints, the most ancient discovery of fire, of clothing and shelter, of the healing properties of herbs, of the wheel and the bow, are all fruits of ingenuity, the elements of a scientific attitude.

But it does seem that for science to come into its own, human beings must be able to sit back and look about them with a certain measure of detachment and impartiality; primitive man was too involved, too beaten down by crippling material servitudes to indulge in the patient observation and methodical analysis and the recording of data that alone make science possible. So it is that science only appears in high civilizations which have found a way of providing resources to spare and so of enabling some men to attend to activities that are rarely immediately remunerating.

Science was quite advanced in ancient China, as it was among the Arabs. In Europe, the revival of learning which came with the Renaissance, and a combination of fortunate natural circumstances, enabled scientific investigations to be pursued as never before. Expediency gave way to an organized exploitation of the usually concealed resources of nature. It is trite enough to say that industrialism is the application of scientific discovery through technology, yet many people are not clearly aware that as the spirit of the Renaissance made science possible, so the rise of science was bound to bring about a quite fundamental change in human life which has been loosely called the industrial revolution, and that furthermore, since science and technology advance apace, industrialism becomes a self-perpetuating and developing process. There can be absolutely no halt, no reversal to it, and no compromise of the past with it. It is an entirely synthetizing, special and independent process,[19] respecting nothing, changing all.

Industrialism has infiltrated into every aspect of life; nothing exists that has not behind it some vast industrial ramification. Even the humble potato is the result of a giant chemical fertilizer industry, not to mention pest control, mechanized marketing, deep freeze, plastic wrappings. Those who still take life to be much the same as it has always been, believing that nature is still somewhere there in the remaining expanses of the countryside, in the scattered forests, ignore the brutal fact that industrial involvement extends to every acre of land today in the advanced industrial countries. Only sentimental blinkers prevent people from seeing that industrialism is essentially anti-nature, mercilessly and systematically; what it cannot dismiss and remove, it ravages. It can but proceed by synthesis.

If these remarks concern today but a third of the world, its most prosperous and active portion, there is an ever-increasing, world-wide recruitment to industrialism, and it is inevitable that industrialism shall proceed till the entire planet is one vast industrial society. One should have the courage to face the implications of it to the full. Ours is likely to be a completely denatured planet in a relatively short period of time, and many of the marks and separations of human existence today will have been dissolved by this planetary phenomenon.

Industrialism as culture

The spirit of classicism was always disdainful of the upstart science, although, when science promised order and human aggrandisement, classicism accepted it temporarily. The rise of science, and the fundamental reversal of human existence that this has involved, are now seen by the classicist in his modern survivals as a denial of humanism and good order. The opposition to science is remarkably active still, accentuated today in many people by the more ominous threats of atomic annihilation. A curious schizoid attitude prevails. While many accept avidly the fruits of science, in the products of industry, they are antiscientific in feeling, and the notion that science, and industrialism in general, are anti-cultural is very prevalent. It is felt to be something that is now necessary, but it is not culture.

The truth of the matter is that science and industrialism have shattered the roots of the previously established cultural patterns and ways of thinking, feeling, and believing, and demands for change are always resisted. Culture there is, but of quite a different kind, culture which is not yet clearly out of the womb and not aware of its differences and distinctions.

Yet the drawing away of the people from the land into urban and industrial living so that today only some 5 per cent of the population of a country like England is engaged in agriculture, has produced a human type so different as to constitute a new cultural species. This is not an empty play with words, for what can make men meet as men but communication at a level of common responses? The differences today between the last remainders of the uncontaminated peasantries and the people of the highly industrialized countries is so marked as to be a barrier not only to social contact, but even to breeding.

The preatomic phase

The industrial revolution obtains its strength and momentum by the ruthless breaking into of nature's hordes of energy, first of all the easily available ones which come from agitations in the outer core of the atom, in the electronic outerhouse, in such sources of energy as fire, coal and oil. The development of the industrial revolution from Watt's steam engine to the close of the thirties can be accounted for as a progressive increase in making use of that same outerhouse of atomic energy. No new energies are tapped, and it was foreseen that there must come in time an end to such progress. In 1935 one could look forward to a much better utilization of natural resources, more efficient production and better sharing and socialization of world wealth, but an end to it was even then in sight. The limitations of human power remained, and it is this more than anything else that marks out the first phase of the industrial revolution, which can be said to reach its end in the most efficient thermal engines and internal combustion engines and in the most efficient development of production in mass methods and automation. Man, in spite of all his progress, was tapping no newer energies than Sinanthropus had used in his fires close on a million years before.[20]

This first phase has a distinct bearing on culture. The realization of man's limited powers prevented a complete and total severance with the past and with nature. One can see an example of this lingering dependence in the attitude of an architect like Lloyd Wright; his belief that the ultimate salvation of industrial civilization would come in a subtle compromise with a nature that had been too hastily discarded. The vision that man could, by his entire synthesis, completely dispense with nature seemed too far a stretch, and the art of this preatomic phase, although in advanced abstraction, has still a definite streak of nature-retention in it, of a nostalgia for its supports and emotional comforts in the midst of an environment all too frequently hostile and inhuman.

The naturalisms of Abstract Impressionism and of the totally geometric image have been pointed out. Among poets, it is even clearer; nature remains a continual emotional reference. There are practically no nature-independent poets to this day. The synthetic world is avoided, if not openly rejected, by many intellectuals, and music itself does not go beyond a highly mutilated impressionism in composers like Schönberg. Man flies with ease, and he has made many remarkable things, and he will no doubt make many more, but he is still a highly altered, even a mutilated version of nature-man; he still cherishes his gardens and his flowered wallpapers. In his cities, he struggles to retain his squares and his parks, and his windowboxes bear the vestiges of his lost floral glory. The antinature inherent in industrialism has not completely won.

There can be little doubt that had science not found the way of breaking into the intra-atomic hordes of energy, a final and total freedom from nature would have been impossible, and the 'Traditional Modern' painting would have remained for an endless future as the most advanced and the most appropriate. There would have been little call for a radically new painting, entirely synthetic and absolutely independent of nature.

The post-atomic age

Although the discovery of atomic energy is very recent, barely a quarter of a century—and the new painting is barely older—there were indications that man could break out of his ancient energy limitations at the beginning of the century. The equating of mass with energy in Einstein's relativity meant, theoretically at least, that stupendous energy could be got from matter. As early as 1921 Lord Haldane had suggested that one day atomic energy would be harnessed, but this realization only came after the experimental research of Fermi and others.

As is known today, virtually unlimited energy is now not only theoretically, but practically, available, an increase of several billionfold compared to the utmost use of the previous atomic outerhouse. One can understand that this is likely to involve a cultural alteration utterly drastic and revolutionary, although the implications are not yet widely appreciated. People need ladders for imagination to work, and the human mind collapses in trying to foresee what can and will be done with the energy now available. Patterns of thought effective in the Renaissance are still current, even among scientists. Yet virtually any fantasy that the mind can conjure is realizable—if and when will depend entirely on the abilities of human beings to remain human and to use this fantastic new power wisely, on human endeavour and ingenuity.

Anyone who doubts the near-miraculous openings which have been explored by science fiction, should read the following passage, not at all fiction, but factual deductions from the theory of relativity.[21]

> The crew of a spaceship moving relative to the earth at a speed approaching the velocity of light . . . the life of the crew appears to the terrestrial observer to be extended as their speed approaches the velocity of light, like the life of the Immortals; they can thus survive many generations of earth dwellers. Despite this, the crew has no sensation of living differently or more slowly than on earth; the slowing down of time on board the rocket, as seen by the terrestrial observer, can only become apparent to them when they return to this observer and compare calendars. This stretching of proper time on board the spaceship . . . produces the important effect that the spaceship can, in a few rocket years and with a reasonable size of rocket, cover distances which the terrestrial observer measures in millions of light years. . . .

Human beings of a not very distant future will be able to move mountains, create new continents, and build entire cities under the oceans. An entirely synthetic environment and a total dispensing with nature has at last become possible, and indeed inevitable, and it is this that makes the postatomic age so very different from the earlier phases of the industrial revolution; its culture, its art, is bound to be very different. If a questioning of man's wisdom in abandoning nature could have been excused in the earlier days of the industrial revolution, there can be no doubt at all of the potential splendour of it now; it can be the means of man's godlike metamorphosis.

Thanks to this breakthrough, man's most pressing problem is no longer likely to be primarily materialistic; the overriding problem that now faces man is how this new synthetic world is to be made compatible with the limits of human acceptability, physiological and emotional, and how human beings can manage to remain human with the most ancient reminders of humanism in nature completely dispensed with, a problem on which art has a great deal to say.

The last revolution

Fantastic as may be the prospects ahead, it is well to realize that the break into the atomic hoards of energy is the last possible break. This is something that has often been said before, but now it is almost certainly true, for the only possibility that remains is the actual creation of matter and energy, a possibility to be dismissed at present as outside the human reckoning.

It follows from this that as the first steam engine was the prototype of the most elaborate turbine, here and now the prototypes of a future of unspecifiable duration are in all the bounds of possibility being worked out and laid down, and this in all fields of cultural activity, in art as much as in science.

The developments of science and of technology take time, and it may not be possible today to sense the lines of future development,[22] but in the emotional realms of the mind there need be no such delay. Intuition is direct and immediate and can rapidly find the ways and means to its revelation, in word, in music, in painting. Within a generation or two new ways of expression can be found to germinate unconscious reactions within human society to a changed environment. This is what one would expect from an animal primarily emotional and only subsequently rationalizing. So it is quite possible that the prototypes of the art of the post-atomic age—an age, one must emphasize, of unforeseeable termination—are already among us. In looking for the newest imageries of the present age, we may well be finding the kind of art that is likely to persist for a very long time.

We have become used to sensational changes in art and a continuous string of novelty. But it is possible that this phase is coming to an end. We have lived through the last great revolution. Real revolutions are anyway exceedingly rare. What has seemed revolution in the past now turns out to have been alteration, drastic and confusing, of the traditional and pre-established system. When one reflects that the realist prototypes of the entire Renaissance, which continued its development into nineteenth-century materialism in science and realism in painting, was laid down in the fourteenth century, and that there were five hundred years of manifold variety and alteration but no fundamental break, one should be more prepared to accept that what lies ahead now is not so much continued revolution, as variability, exploitation, mutation, fusions, and divisions.

But before passing to these new imageries let us have a look at this science that has brought about this real and final revolution in human existence, and which is in one way and another responsible for radically altered reactions to life and living. We shall indeed find in this survey of science a revolution as acute as any in human life. The science that ushered in the industrial revolution of the first phase has radically changed itself, and when one notes the extent of the change, not only in science but in every human field, in life as much as in art, one can but come to the conclusion that our civilization is in a state of crisis and impending drastic change as severe, as pregnant with risk and prospect, as occurred when the Renaissance reversed the medieval heritage. Indeed, incomparably more risk, and unimaginably wider prospects.

4

THE NEW AGE: REVOLUTION
IN SCIENCE

B Y the close of the nineteenth century the successes of science
had made a deterministic rationalism the common sharing
of all educated people. Phenomena which could not be
accounted for by science were considered either delusional, the
results of wrong looking or plain wishful thinking. With such a
world view, culture itself could only be a matter of social organization and control, of precise information and education, of knowledge, in fact, and the part which art could be called upon to play
in such a scheme was quite a minor one.

It is one of the strangest ironies, which many scientists still find
it hard to accept, that methods and approaches based on a firm
belief in an ultimate materiality and precision of natural laws have
uncovered a certain inconsistency in the natural order. The
'elementary particles' which compose the atoms of matter are not
basically particulate in a solid, impenetrable sense. In one aspect
of their existence they are wave-like, a state of things which it is
not possible to conceptualize.[23]

Passing from microphysics to the cosmological scale, the
theories of relativity imply the abandonment of fixed invariable
references, and a new inconceivable agency, space-time, becomes
the dynamic substitute. Fixed references were essential requirements for a precise, deterministic approach to natural phenomena.
Relativism is incompatible with a static, precisely analysable and
immutable view of things. Although the gross behaviour of
countless billions of atoms in chunks and pieces of what we
commonly call matter does average out and so allows massive
phenomena to comply with the laws of classical physics, matter in
its ultimate and therefore most real condition is quite incompatible
with those laws. At the very heart of things there is a degree of
imprecision, which is not the result of bad instruments, or wrong

seeing, but is an incorrigible quality of things in themselves. At the best, science is now limited to a statistical treatment rather than a pinpointing of final and irrevocable facts.

It is important to realize that there is no passage from classical physics to modern physics. If a virus or even a group of molecules under the electron microscope casts a shadow just like a billiard-ball, and would be best portrayed by the traditional techniques of realist art, when one comes to the tremulous fields of force between molecules and atoms, or to energy tracks, one is dealing with quite a different imagery for which the traditional techniques of painting are useless. The only conclusion possible is that the view of classical physics has in one sense omitted an aspect of reality, and that the precision and determinism it aspired to and found in the large pieces of matter was in truth illusional. Basic reality is quite different. There is no passage from the one to the other, for the simple reason that as soon as we realize the illusion the firmness of reality disappears.

There can be no doubt that this conclusion amounts to a profound cultural shock, for our entire culture has been based, since the Renaissance, on a confidence in material finality and reliability. It does not really help to say that the traditional laws still apply at the practical level of things: science, and human thinking, must face the truth of the underlying situation. A proof that what happens in science affects human beings not only at practical levels, but at the level of intimate thought, emotion, and reaction, is seen in the spread of this shock into very wide fields. Not only philosophers and sociologists have been affected by it, but critics, poets, psychologists, and it has even appeared in the novel and the play.

In coping with this discomfiting situation, science has been obliged to have recourse to a variety of symbolic languages, for, if a precise and definite approach is no longer feasible, only circumnavigation and allusion remain possible. This is a happening which should bring great comfort to the arts. Only yesterday, science was deriding the symbolic mode as unrealistic and inconsequential, as it must indeed be in a world which is nothing but precise and deterministic, whereas now science itself is adopting procedures which have been eternally practised by the arts—the manipulation of the symbolic.

As art could tell science, reality is elusive and imprecisable, and the quest for a final seizing of it is the proof of a psychological infirmity. Reality is double-faced and paradoxical. If the new physics has its way of saying this in Heisenberg's Principle, so the new paintings have theirs, and so have the new writing and the new music. There is no question of borrowings and unrealized influence here. Although there has been a diffusion of the scientific crisis in a wide field, the phenomenon in the arts is too fundamental to be derivative. It can but be what Sir Charles Snow has aptly termed the wide-scale correlation, the response of an entire culture to changed conditions. The idea that science itself is quite uninfluenced by the ways of life and the climate of thought is simply not true, for scientific theories are popular or unpopular in good part according as to whether they happen to fit in with the prevalent climate of feeling. As many a pioneer in science has known, even facts are resisted if there is not such a fit. When the conditions are right, all the aspects of a culture, practical, intellectual, and emotional, find themselves working out along more or less parallel lines.

Scientists are, of course, human, and nothing but human, and one must expect a ferocious resistance to this demand for drastic revisions and adjustments. Quite a few have spent abounding energy in attempting to prove that this is simply not so, that the old order still prevails. Pavlov's conditioned reflexes affect more than the individual; the concept applies to a culture. We have all of us conditioned reflexes as to how we should think, what we should believe. Yet the facts of the crisis are there, as undeniable as an open wound.

It should be no surprise that reason has its limits, for, as a faculty, it has been evolved to function and do service at a very particular level of things in the cosmic hierarchy, the level of gross, piecemeal happenings, and it has been the evolutionary role of our senses to insist that reason is unique and paramount, else reason would never have evolved out of the primordial emotionalism. Reason can but strive to make itself exclusive. Why indeed should the Universe have stopped at reason and matter? Unless one is to assume a most provident organization that the Universe should limit itself to the range of human understanding!

It is a curious fact that the materialists who insist on a consistently understandable material orderliness are committing an act of faith as immense as the theologians in their view that this is the best of all possible worlds. It is surely more consistent to admit that the Universe is more than can be conveniently seized by human reason while yet in no way denying its self-subsistent orderliness.

The extension of the Universe beyond what we choose to call matter is indeed the most natural and expectable of things. But the appearance of the faculty of reason, which has been evolved to tell us that only reasonable relations are real, puts us in a situation of paradox. It is not so much the Universe that is paradoxical; it is the inherent limitation of man's main weapon to knowledge and understanding that forces a conceptual break and so produces what can but seem a paradox.

The situation of paradox, however, means that an 'either-or' logic—that a thing can only be one thing or the other, but never both—fails. It is, like determinism, a misconception that arises out of the static view of things. It is only reason that sees such drastic revisions of view and attitude as limiting; a Universe that cannot be accurately defined, that cannot be seized and fixed and categorized, cherished as these actions may be by rational thinking, is a Universe of endless becoming, a Universe dynamic and alive, incomplete, ceaseless, and one should see that, in the long run, it is this view which is extensive, and the static view demanded by reason which is limiting.

Science fifty years ago had set out to find out all there was to know in the Universe, and believed that it could do it; such an arrogance has been corrected, but man can still acquire knowledge, and experience of things. If a final, dead fact is ruled out, the trembling truth of the symbol remains; man has the most ancient devices of dialectic, of allusion, of metaphor and parable,[24] adapted to modern uses, and new symbolic metamathematical systems, to help him; and he has art. Once again, art becomes as legitimate a way of knowing as science. It is a striking realization that whereas reason emerged out of a primitive emotionalism and tended to supplant its symbolic revelations, greater wisdom and understanding have obliged man to return to the way of knowledge which emotionalism first of all opened up to him. Reality, an eternally imprecisable condition, is coming to be seen by all ways of approach as closer to the ancient view of art than to the view of a deterministic science.[25]

Art shows vividly that the abandonment of a precise, deterministic, calculated approach does not bring in chaos necessarily, but can be succeeded by a quite new and different order. Art also shows that this does not mean a total and entire indeterminism; that surely can but mean irrationalism. It means a relativistic, opportunistic determinism or indeterminism. Systems and regularities remain, study is possible, choice is inevitable, but finality is ruled out.

It is exceedingly difficult for the inquiring mind to reach even a rough approximation of this state of affairs. Some, like Capek, have maintained that any visualization is quite impossible, and he provides an analogy in music. The freedom to improvise in jazz today, as in certain parts of classical music, shows that pre-existent, determined order is not necessary, that an opportunistic, dynamic order is attained in the course of actualization. But if the static, deterministic image of traditional art cannot provide a visual analogy, the new painting can, for here we have much the same thing in visual terms, an absence of intention, yet the realization of dynamic order.

As the Universe is dynamic, and not closed and finished, it is inevitable that precision should be impossible, just as it is impossible to get a sharp photograph of a fast-moving object. In an interesting manner, a look at the 'substance' of mental imagery provides a vivid analogy of this imprecisability. In imagination, images are fluid. Although one may have the impression that one knows a person's face minutely, as soon as we try to draw it we find that this is not so: the feeling of certainty was not physical, but emotional, and it was the smoky, elusive symbol of it that provided us with a feeling of minute knowledge. This fluidity is especially noticeable in the conceptualizing processes that go on in poetry and writing. Quoting de Sanctis as cited by Sir Herbert Read,[26] 'When a subject comes into the brain of a creative writer, it at once dissolves the part of reality which suggested it; the earthly messages seem to fluctuate, like objects in a mass of vapour. . . .'

This analogy is instructive, for we see that the task of the artist is to give some degree of fixity to the symbolic situation. It must neither be so incoherent that it loses all structure, nor must it be so determined as to lose an essential ambiguity; the object in art is like a ball on a jet of water. And one sees that what the rationalizing mind, and a deterministic science tend to bring about is just this peeling away of the skins of ambiguity till only a sharp, definite image is left, an image that may well suit the practical purposes of life and a pragmatic science, but it is not a proper view of reality and is opposed to the view of art.

The dynamic approach of the new science has not in any way reduced the importance of experiment. On the contrary, rather than intellectual theory-building, it is the dynamic constellation of as many facts as can be amassed that meets with the present statistical, analogical approach. So it is in art. A static view of art, with fixed external references, could be built up methodically to a state of ultimate perfection; with no external references, and with the view that a work of art is not a finalized thing but only an aspect of an ambiguous process, assay, continual and unceasing, is the only creative procedure, and success or failure cannot be known till afterwards. This character of opportunistic experimentalism alone makes the new art radically different from all that has gone before.

The change from a science of observation to a science of synthesis has a bearing on art. Earlier science was concerned with observation, experiments with existing entities, and classification, whereas the new science has passed over to actual creation in synthesis. The recent cracking of the genetic code in cells is likely to lead to the actual creation of living systems. The importance of this change is immense. If, only a century ago, man was content to strive to know nature, now he is intent on outdoing nature, and one sees that this is one aspect of the anti-nature drive evident in technology and industry. The spirit of synthesis is particular to the present phase of industrial civilization, and thanks to it, man will in time completely dispense with nature. As it is, he is producing synthetic replacements of materials, on which men have been entirely dependent for thousands of years, far superior on every count. The move from a dependence on nature in the arts to synthesis, which is the most critical feature of all the valid imageries today, is another instance of wide-scale cultural correlation.

But if one were to pick out any general cultural feature typical of the present phase, it would be the tendency to penetration on all fronts. In science, this began by a physical penetration, made possible by improved instruments, by microscopes and telescopes and cloud-chambers. Also in painting it began by a physical penetration, in the Impressionists' analysis of vision. But the underlying force is intellectual, even emotional, and is due to a particular cultural attitude. Modern man is simply not satisfied with appearances, and this dissatisfaction is the direct result of a complex cultural evolution. Psychology, and its concern with the unconscious, could have developed a century before; the unconscious was there as always, but the inner drive to penetration was lacking. An awareness of the unconscious is also tied up with a certain neurotic self-examination and restlessness of the mind that goes with an artificializing civilization in general, and it is this that has obliged man to expand his view of the physical Universe beyond immediate reason, to grope for new concepts of the mind beyond mechanism, and in the arts, to move towards an abstract autonomy.

The consequences of this are enormous. To the classical, Renaissance mind up to its survivals in nineteenth-century materialism, utmost clarity of statement and vision were aspects of the quest for precision and rigid determinism. Physical penetration in science has shown that reality is not finally precisable, that there is an inherent fluidity and ambiguity in all things which can never be overcome, and psychological penetration has taught the same thing in the realm of the mind. The Cartesian spirit in painting, still evident in most of the painters of the Ecole de Paris, looked upon conciseness, precision, and simplicity as virtues in themselves. Simplicity in particular has been especially hailed as one of the aims and delights of art. It is true that a simple visual statement is easier to accept, visually and aesthetically, but according to a virtual law, it is also all the easier to empty and exhaust emotionally. The growing respect for imprecision and ambiguity in the imageries of the new painting means that simplicity and clarity are abandoned, and that a certain 'opacity' and functional complexity are more essential virtues. This, of course, does not mean unnecessary complicatedness; the complexity must be real and have in itself symbolic meaning, and if this makes the new painting much less easy to approach, it does ensure a far greater symbolic wealth.

This functional complicatedness is very important in the visual arts. It is the main technical means of creating a sense of ambiguity. A clear, simple statement can but be a determinate one, tending towards Euclidean relationships, whereas a jumble of lines is much more apt to break into a quite different symbolic world. If given structure, then the result will be some new kind of ambiguous geometry.

The classical, traditional mind is only too likely to condemn this as chaos, yet if prejudice can be laid aside, it does open up into a new world of ambivalent experience, and if the painter can achieve this functional, meaningful complexity by intuitive means, it is also possible to arrive at it by a more calculated approach. This might appear to amount to a contradicition of what has already been said, but it is not so. If a thing is *seen* as ambiguous, it is this that matters to the onlooker, not the method whereby this ambiguity was obtained. It is not suggested that the painter should produce his results by more or less intended complexity, but it is important in fields where control over materials is much more difficult and indeed impossible without calculation and predetermination, as in architecture.

One can now realize that perhaps the main cause of failure of the traditional approach, in art as in science, is the attempt to simplify, and the belief that in such simplifying, nothing is lost; the old, old view that the entire world is there and only waiting for man's most limited understanding to reveal all its secrets to him. This simpleton attitude has had, as one can expect, the most disastrous consequences in those phenomena which are the most complex and which owe most of their characteristics to their complexity, as in living things.[27] There is a growing respect in the sciences for organicism, integrated, self-maintaining and adjusting systems which do not allow unnecessary interruption for the conveniences of study. This is perhaps the supreme quality of art, which makes the difference between a jumble and a proper work of art, and here a science like biology, which deals with more complicated levels of organization, is providing even physics with certain concepts. Once again, a cultural correlation on widely different fronts is being realized.[28]

This synchronicity of effort in the new science and the new painting should remove any doubt that science is an all-determining cultural yardstick. It is not, as anti-science tends to claim, simply a convenient supplier of goods and discoveries, and so must be kept in its place. It is the agency of the times that every artist who wishes to be truly contemporary should take good note of, and a closer look at some of the individual sciences can but be profitable for the present purpose.

Physics

Still influenced by the ideals of classical unity, all his life Einstein endeavoured to find a unitary key to his theories, which would have made relativity subordinate to a universal constancy.[29] But relativity remains relative and marks the change from the worldview of the Renaissance. The abandonment of fixed references in art is comparable.

Heisenberg's Principle of Indeterminancy states that the position of an electron and its speed cannot both be accurately defined together, and that, as a result, an irremediable imprecision is a part of nature. In art, a comparable law exists: the more precisely form is defined, the less energy can be symbolized.

Bohr's related Complementarity Principle states that it is impossible to gain a complete and final knowledge of any natural phenomenon, owing to a dynamic double face of reality. Only an approach from a plurality of angles, by statistical sampling, is possible. Furthermore the human observer invariably interferes with any situation or phenomenon as he observes it. The critic I. A. Richards has seen an application of these ideas in the poets grappling with a poetical reality which is fundamentally elusive.

The classical view of the Universe foresaw a balanced,[30] symmetrical order in the 'laws of nature'. An asymmetrical aspect has been recently discovered in microphysics; the matter of the Universe is apparently basically unbalanced, qualitatively and quantitatively. The elemental brick of life, the carbon atom, echoes this fundamental asymmetry, and the underlying dynamics of life, its restless refusal to come to a stop in the evolution of living things, may be traceable to this.[31]

The notion that art should aspire to an ultimate perfection of balanced constituents is typically classical, clearly defined in such formulations as the Golden Mean, and in compositional correlation. The new imageries flaunt such rules; they are often unbalanced, asymmetrical, segmental, or centrifugal, and the word composition itself has largely lost its meaning. It can only apply to static, deterministic arrangements, not to the dynamic.

It is becoming realized that all things operate by a dynamic dialectic, and the mere presence of one thing tends to evoke something opposite to it; the more emphatic and successful it is, then the more this becomes apparent, a principle one finds confirmed not only in science and in life, but in art. One realizes also that this sort of oscillation is quite unimaginable from a static view of things, but a thing which is fundamentally imprecisable and unbalanced can be either one thing or the other, and, in a new sense and when viewed from a particular standpoint, something of both. An appearance of 'one-thingness' is an illusion.

So one sees that if matter perforce must be faced with anti-matter, form by its apparent denial in energy, so creation in art is likely to be faced by destruction, art by anti-art. It is significant that in an examination of all the valid techniques today, one can espy a degree of destructiveness coupled with creativeness.

Mathematics and logic

With Bacon, Newton, and Descartes, the Renaissance confidence in the reliability of the material order found apparent irrevocable confirmation in mathematical systems of absolute clarity, precision, and a total absence of contradiction and ambiguity. Mathematics appeared as the highest aspiration of the Age of Reason, and many artists in the Renaissance took a keen interest in it, and were, in fact, able mathematicians, Leonardo, Mantegna, Verrocchio, Piero della Francesca. The ideal traditional image became a kind of mathematical formulation in visual terms, notably in perspective, in formal arrangements and balance. From Liebniz, all the sciences aspired to the precision of mathematics, but in 1931 Godël showed that any mathematical system is bound to contain certain unprovable premises, a demonstration that has come as a profound shock to the deterministic sciences.[32]

In logic, there have been attempts to find exits out of the Aristotelian impasse which has been the basis of traditional logic and which stipulates that a thing can only be one thing or the other, never both. This seems obvious enough to the reasoning mind, but one can imagine that in dynamic systems this need no longer apply; a dynamic system may be built up of the interplay of two opposed events, in situations that can take both ambiguity and paradox seriously.[33] One can see an analogy of this in a piece of fast-moving machinery; composed of quite different and opposite parts, the rapid motion generates a new entire visual experience, an analogy which is pertinent to the fundamental difference between the static imageries of traditional painting and the new dynamic paintings of today.

Cybernetics and information theory

The computer is a dramatic extension of the calculating brain, and it is therefore not at all surprising that a study of it can provide useful hints as to how the human brain itself works.[34]Computation is one of the ways in which the brain functions, not only in man, but in animals.

So far, computers have only been designed to be entirely deterministic and to aid the deterministic functions of the brain, in calculation and correlation, in selection and data storing. Such computers could easily be made to create original deterministic art; traditional music has a strong deterministic core in its symbolic structure, and computers have, in fact, composed quite satisfactory music of this kind. Recent trends towards atonalism and free serialism would put such a computer in a quandary, and no computer exists today that could cope with the ambiguities and imprecisions which are characteristic of the new painting.

But it is possible that an 'analogical' computer will be designable, extending the functions of the mind at the borderlands of conscious awareness. Such a computer might well be one way of getting to know more about the mind, as well as about the more elusive phenomena of art. It would be the only means of creating a 'free' piece of music or an autonomous image which would retain a symbolic ambiguity.

Man is a communicating animal; self-communication is being alive, communicating to others the assertion of one's livingness. Up to now, scientists have been chiefly concerned with factual communication, but studies in cybernetics, in information storing, selecting and transmitting systems, in autoregulative and self-adjusting systems in machines and chemical systems, all involving advanced electronics, as well as the methods of operational research, are enormously extending the horizons of human communication. Years of human knowing can be crowded into a few microseconds of an electronic operation, years of visual outfolding on a few grams of video-tape.[35]

The ancient limitations of time and space are virtually overcome in the new aids to knowledge and understanding, and it is possible to conceive that a quite new level of understanding, outside the human brain and mind, can be created, which will be able to extend human experience beyond its present physiological and neural limitations. It is a brutal fact that we are often apt to forget in our reach for the stars that the speed of a nervous impulse along a nerve goes at the very slow rate of eighty miles an hour!

Astronomy and cosmology

Even more than physics, traditional astronomy saw life as something utterly remote and uncongenial in a precise material Universe. Like all the sciences, astronomy has itself become penetrative by quite remarkable technical means, and has in fact,, penetrated into the interior of suns and stars. Instead of purely accidental theories, evolutionary concepts have taken over, and planets are coming to be seen as a natural and inevitable part of stellar evolution, and it is now widely believed that, far from an accidental exception, life is common throughout the Universe. As Hoyle has remarked, 'somewhere there must be a cricket team that can beat the Australians'. One might add that other planets have had their Leonardos, Cézannes, and Pollocks.

The classical view tends to see the Universe as a 'once for all' creation, moving to some sort of final end, but relativism is coming into astronomy and cosmology in the growing belief that the desire for classical finality is erroneous, that creation is continuous or oscillative. Professor McCrea's recent contention[36] that there is an actual limitation in man's cosmic viewing which cannot possibly be surpassed by any physical means is in tune with a limitation of determinism in all fields. The Universe, far from being the precise mechanical work foreseen in the nineteenth century, may be much closer to a work of art.

Biology

Aristotelian preoccupations with form had made biology a form-ridden science by the close of the nineteenth century. Even the evolution theory, which is surely dynamic, sponsored at first only a static study of organs. Nowhere else does one see so clearly the difficulties inherent in the human brain to think dynamically. But

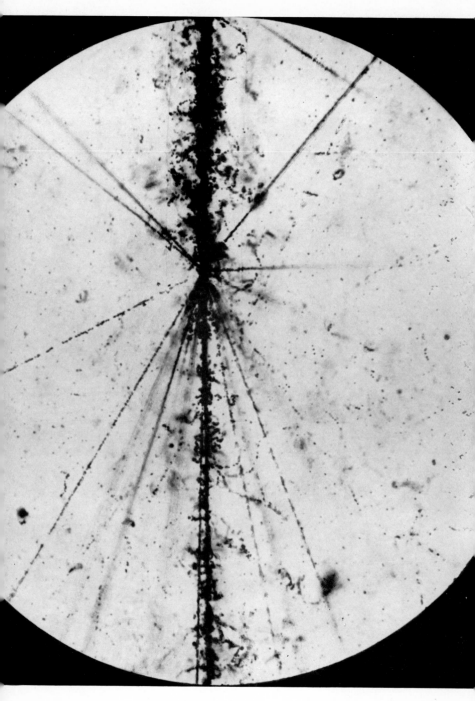

I

2

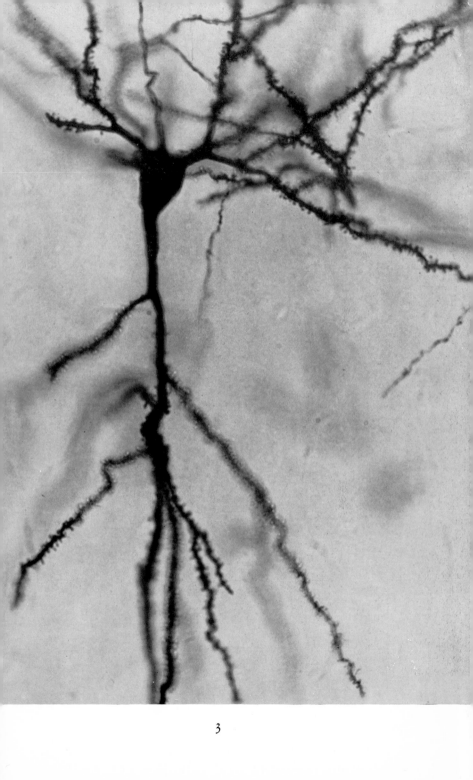

VESUVIUS

SCALE of MILES
0 5 10 20 30 40 50 60 70 80

2 10

5

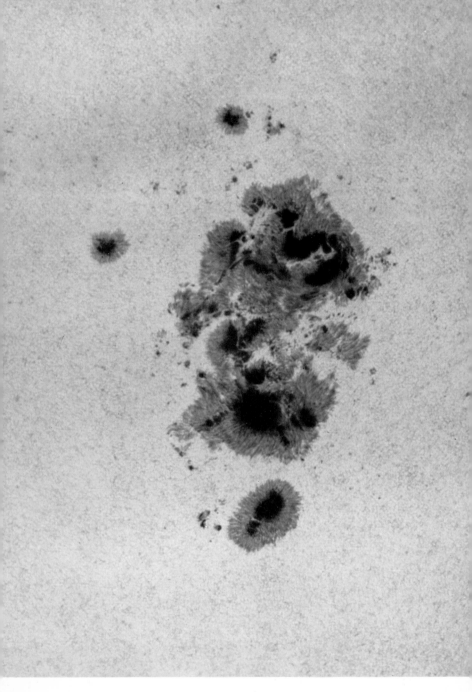

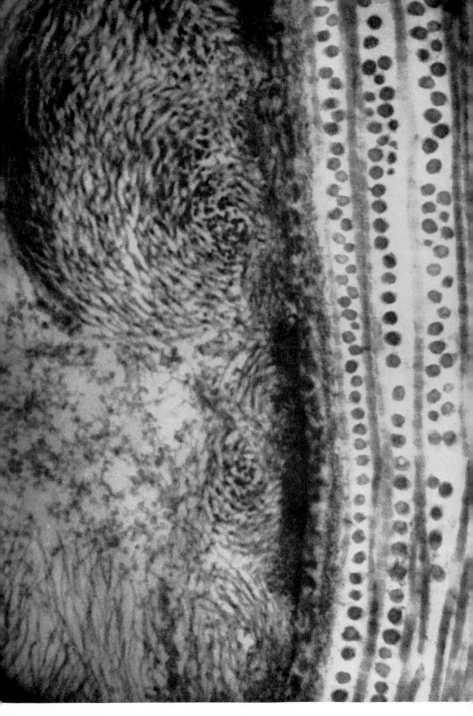

9

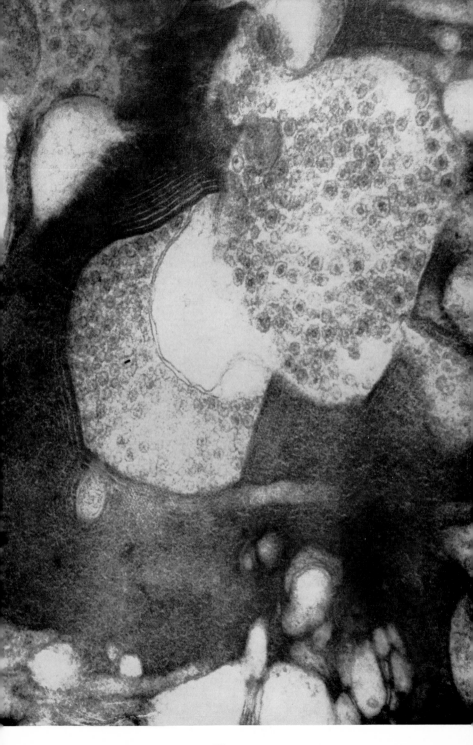

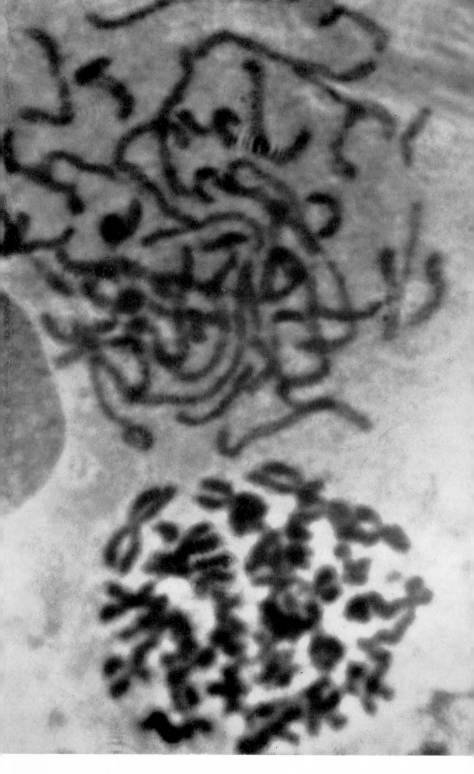

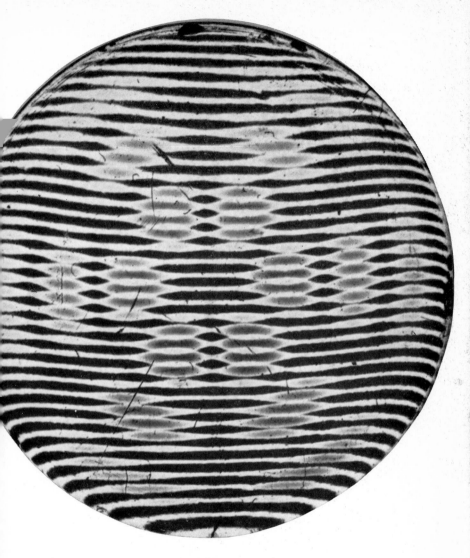

13

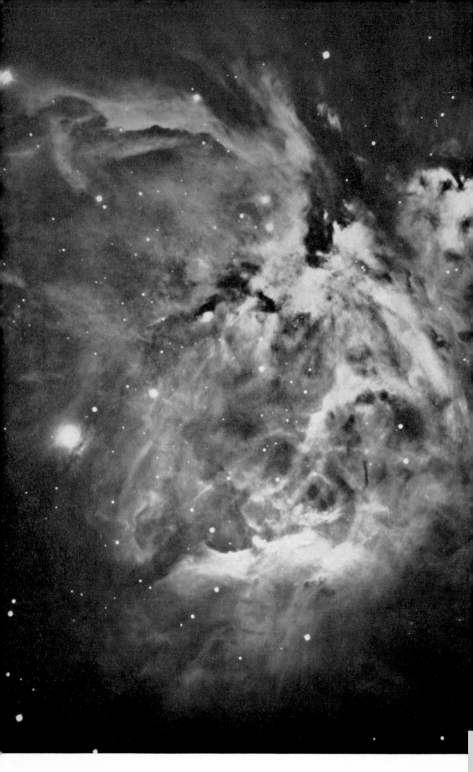

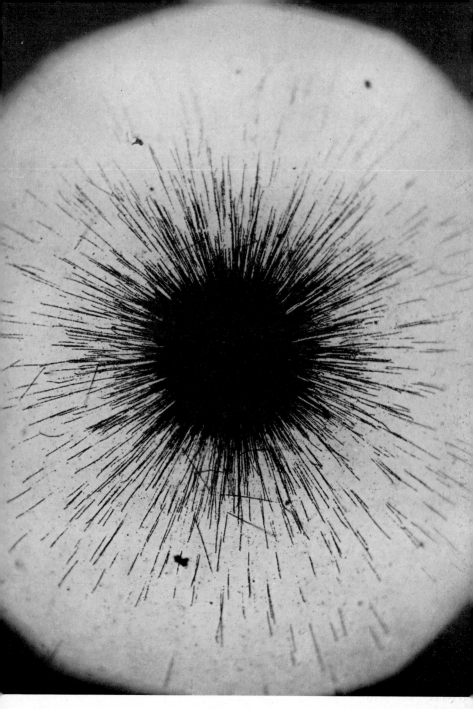

advances in biochemistry and physics have come to correct this, in more organicist, integrative concepts.

Except in the more superficial phenomena of life, simple mechanistic ideas fail; life is life because of its particular dynamic organization,[37] self-adjusting, self-creating, and self-reproducing. Recent interest in autoregulative systems in very complicated machines and in elaborate chemical systems are more relevant, and one sees here again that the simple view popular to reason is quite inadequate. An admission of an irreducible complicatedness becomes necessary.

Like life, art owes its virtues to the fact of its organization. The work of art is matter, but matter organized in a very particular way, that raises it to a supermaterial level. Any attempt to analyse art into purely material components is bound to fail. Only a dynamic study of its organization, overall and integrative, can have any hope of success, and that is altogether more difficult. It is an interesting observation that if simpler machines made by man are purely mechanical, the most complicated machines being made today acquire new characteristics which are analogous to living things. Since the human being can legitimately judge a thing at a purely symbolic level, one can truthfully say that such machines are 'alive', and it is also interesting that such machines evolve, through a process of natural selection, analogous to the evolution of life.[38]

Most of the wrong thinking in biology is due to the culturally enforced errors of a deterministic rationalism. For instance, in the problem of ontology, errors arise in wrong attitudes to time, to direction. Life, as it evolves, is 'open', like music that can be played a very large number of ways; as it evolves it becomes canalized, and order and pattern emerge. Looking back, one sees an apparently deterministic intention, but this is an illusion due to a wrong placing in time; at the actual moment of evolution, the problem is quite different. This is just the case with the creation of a work of art. It does not pre-exist, yet, looking at the product, there is discernible order, form, and apparent intention. Life is inherently a free-wheeling opportunism, and has no doubt evolved in very different ways in other planets, in animals which breathe ammonia instead of oxygen, in the use of silicon instead of carbon, and it is not its actual coursing that matters, but its creation of quite new levels of existence. The emergence of organized matter in the form of life is just such a new level, with new features and characters which did not exist before. So is the emergence of mind, of emotionalism.

One cannot fail to sense a profound relatedness of art to the cosmic process in this observation, for art does exist, as quite a new level, and in a true sense, evolution, in its antientropic level-raisings, can be said to proceed in art as in mind.

Psychology

Like the other sciences, psychology has attempted to be deterministic,[39] but matter-of-fact attempts to account for mind, like those of Ryle and Ayer, and the reliance on the conditioned reflex in Marxist countries, leave out too much. These approaches are right with what they deal with, as there is unquestionably one aspect of mind-function that can be so analysed and accounted for, but they are right only by exclusion and the disregard of a host of inconvenient evidence.

The inadequacies of official psychology have brought into being schools which are fundamentally opposed to such ideas as behaviourism and mechanism, in existential, relativistic psychologies.[40] The error of seeing the mind as one thing and the brain as another, and the materialistic obligation of dismissing the mind as a result, stems from the same cultural bigotry that has sought to find a static, final, and deterministic material order in physics. As physicists like Dirac[41] have suggested, both physics and psychology may well spring as different specializations from some sort of common 'substratum' which is not properly in space and time and which can account both for the properties of matter and of mind. Sir George Thomson[42] has suggested that the microstructure of the brain cells is so fine that it may well be subject to the Principle of Indeterminancy, and events not properly in material space and time may run in intimate correspondence to produce the evident synchronization of thought, of feeling, of brain and body. Some such provision would enable occasional strange experiences, like those explored by an experimental parapsychology, to be accepted in an all-embracing view of nature.[43]

The physicist Pauli and the psychologist Jung[44] suggested a comparable synchronicity between physical events and mental events, enabling an overrun of the one and the other in such phenomena as telekinesis and foresight, as well as in ordinary memory. The error of seeing the individual mind as one thing and an external world as another is an error born of an artificial set of human senses, that gives a practically useful view of things but one which is fundamentally deceiving. In some sort of universal extension, not properly or entirely within space and time, Bohr's claim that the observer interferes actively in the material phenomenon observed finds a better explanation.

The emotionalized inner world of man appears as a mind within a mind, another and quite distinct level of mental attainment. Its origins in the course of evolution in the emotionalization of sex, and its fundamental difference from the physiological, physical, and cerebral because of man's special sex needs have already been mentioned. This fundamental difference makes it a quite new human extension, and if it has been made discreet and uninterfering, man's conquest over material need is likely to enable it to evolve into more explicit, evident, and active forms. Art is the means of its visible exercise, and although it is not possible to imagine concretely in what directions such an evolution could lead, it is here and now a singular and superior attainment of creative evolution.

Although orthodox psychologies have done much to make the 'other' order of art an accepted fact, there have been few attempts[45] to account for the elusive and less precisable aspects of mind evident in art. A psychology, quite special and distinct, of human emotionalism has become necessary, and the evidences which art offers, and which cannot be properly accounted for by orthodox psychological ideas, are bound to influence general psychology, and point to the break with materialism and determinism.

Philosophy

The reversal of deterministic rationalism in philosophy has come in our time with Existentialism, and the change from a static, absolute pursuit with the philosphers of change, Spencer, James, Bergson, and especially Whitehead. The change has not been easy or pleasant, for traditional philosophy has been dogged in its pursuit of final causes and references. Relativism and dynamism run right against academic thinking and feeling. The selling out of a large number of schools at the close of the nineteenth century to science has left philosophy high and dry in its defence of a waning static order.

Since Existentialism scorns many of the favoured attitudes and intellectual activities of academic philosophers,[46] it has been accused by many of them of not being philosophy at all. Its recourse to the novel and the play, and its relish in the confusing, opaque statement, are viewed with professional horror. Yet many a poet, writer, and artist have felt a quickening in its reading, in its unmasking of the limitations and false pretences of reason, in its dismissal of classical 'essence' and its revival of a grip with actual life which many academic philosophies appeared to have lost. But it is true that no Existentialism has suggested a methodical approach to human knowledge, capable of correlating all its many and diverse fields, which is still a challenge, and it may be wrong in assuming that this is impossible.

If a philosophy based on now obsolete scientific notions can but fail to do this service, there is a rising possibility for a philosophy that will take into account the recent revolution in science itself. The end of an exclusive reliance on an analytical deterministic rationalism, as we have kept on repeating, is not the end of all orderly treatment. But if metaphysics is dead—the very word suggests a preoccupation with essence which is now intolerable— so are the various survivals of the traditional view in pseudo-modern dress, in various forms of materialism, in logical positivism, in linguistic analysis, and so on.

Marxism as a philosophy, although the first to bring in the idea of a dynamic dialectic in practical existence, has remained nineteenth-century in many of its present applications, and traditional in many of its concepts. Attempts to force it to cover the entire field of human thought and action, and to force it against the growing evidence of recent times, has produced vast stretches of parched thinking not unlike the profusions of the scholastics. Marxist philosophers, like all traditional philosophers,[47] appear to have a singular capacity for unrelated and remote thinking.[48] It is not that Marxism has not made important contributions to modern thought and to the present world-view: it has, in stressing the importance of the social condition, of the place of man in society and history, of the importance of environment, and in the cardinal importance of science itself. But it has shown a strange and disquieting lack of elasticity and ability to modify itself and serve new growing ideas.

Sociology and History

From Spengler and Marx, it has been assumed that, with appropriate knowledge and adequate control, human existence could be deterministically organized and properly directed according to criteria of good and justice. No doubt that this can to some extent be done, but there have been protests that the so-called laws of history and sociology are misleading, the old case of being wise after the event, and that they are essentially misleading in any attempt at organizing the future precisely, for there is a measure of inbuilt indeterminism in man, and therefore in history and society.[49] One is here faced with the recurring struggle as to the absoluteness of reason, or its limitation, and the discussion of this subject is never quite impartial.

But the implication that to admit this indeterminism makes control of human destiny a mockery and makes the scientific treatment of such subjects as history, sociology, and economics impossible, is patently untrue. It cannot mean an absolute indeterminism, for the evidence that human life can be affected by effort and organization is there for all to see. It implies a relative indeterminism, which stresses that although effort and organization are partly effective and indeed essential, one must expect a certain measure of free drive and unpredictability in human affairs, and that human freedom is an essential requirement for the full operation of human progress as a result of this inbuilt free-wheeling.

History is not only relatively indeterministic, owing to a fundamental ambiguity in human nature that reason and organization can never completely correct, but to the endless multiplicity of possible interpretations of the facts. It is here that the study of history becomes an art, and no subject shows this possibility of endless reinterpretation as does art history.

Although traditional scientific notions are useless, such ideas as Neumann presented in his Theory of Games are relevant, and have found practical application in economics.[50] They are applicable because they are dynamic and allow a multiplicity and ambiguity of development.

In a rigidly deterministic society, art can have no more place than Plato foresaw for it, or it can only be used for purely political propaganda. Art, in order to be able to perform its functions of emotional reconciliation, of emotional enhancement of life, of experiment and groping, requires a society with an adequate measure of freedom. Direction and organization cannot by the nature of things be precise, there must be an inbuilt elasticity, a degree of functional opportunism so that the new and unexpected can arise and become selected or rejected. This symbolic freedom is at the heart of a living language,[51] in its ability to meet new situations and induce new ideas. A thoroughly precise language would be one bereft of any ability to grow and alter.

Art history and aesthetics

Just as philosophy had sold out to science at the close of the last century, so the study of art had come to rely on an analytical philosophy which was itself crippled by a deterministic science, and we come upon the vast tracts of official art history, a particularly Germanic affair, of inexhaustible learning and cataloguing, the tabulations of events and places and names, the rigorous endeavours to be factual at all costs by relying on established authorities, on quotations, and the repertoire of historical references. At its best, this kind of approach ends with the Traditional Modern painting: it is quite unequipped for dealing with the new.

This traditional way of thinking not only prevents it from dealing with the new, but forces its condemnation. It appears simply not as art at all. And the classicist's bias one finds in traditional art history often shows strong anti-science traits. In spite of hobnobbing with science in order to gain respectability in an age of science, in spite of an apparent preoccupation with facts and the avoidance of fiction, the possible contributions that science could make are curiously ignored. There is in the Beaux-Arts attitude a scoffing at the vulgarities of science, a belief that art is in some sense above it and can have nothing to learn from it. As a result, not only has art history failed to find support from biology, from the less orthodox aspects of psychology, from sociology, from anthropology, but it tends to perpetuate itself in its isolated academicism, and the art teaching that it still sponsors officially in the majority of art schools is blatantly unrelated to an age of science, to industrialism, and to a drastically changed life and society.

As a result of this state of affairs, a generation has come up that is exasperated with a highly learned but usually irrelevant art historicism, and there has been a tendency to dismiss all art history and methodical approaches to the study of art.[52] Art simply 'is', one is told. This attitude betrays the failure to appreciate that if the old methods have to be dismissed, quite new methods are none the less available, in psychology, in biology—some have already been indicated—even in physics, and in such new methods of study as cybernetics, information theory, the effect of drugs, of mental and physical diseases and disturbances on imagery, the new field of comparative aesthetics, and many other suggestions that the new science can make.

5

THE NEW AGE:
ALTERED SENSIBILITIES

MANY people go about their daily lives virtually unaware that human existence has altered drastically in even a decade. A state of emotional anaesthesia appears to be one reaction to the quandaries of fast-changing existence. That this change is ignored is due to the fact that human emotionalism, underlying all feeling, all thinking, all desire, is by design and intention discreet and camouflaged. But in the false belief that reason and materiality are the only realities, emotionalism becomes smothered, and when it tends to erupt, or when conditions tend to provoke it into evidence, it is derided. This is one good reason why art, an emotional provocateur, is disliked in its most effective forms in a materialistic society: only the more ineffective, bland, and undemanding arts can be tolerated.

But hidden and ignored, the emotional undercurrent is in no way dismissed. As long as human beings remain emotionalized animals, the emotional substratum will respond in its silent, secret, and mostly ignored ways to life, to its changes and crises. It is evident enough, in the wide change of response of all people to living in industrial, urban conditions, in the most common thoughts and feelings, habits and motivations, as well as in the highest art.

The physical environment

Although the ice ages came to an end some ten thousand years ago, the inhabitants of the temperate regions lived, until recently, in near-glacial conditions for a good part of the year. The thick clothing and stuffy interiors which this entailed, the poor lighting and the unpleasant smells, led to a paralysing of the surface sensibilities of human beings. New methods of air conditioning are changing this, encouraging a sensuous awareness and the tactile and kinaesthetic possibilities of the human body. Objects are made to carry a handling invitation, materials call to be caressed, and spaces and structures are conceived in terms of the movement of people and things around them and through them.

It is a sad reflection that in spite of being a materialist, Western man has had no respect for matter and for the physical contacts of his own body. This has not only led to a loss of sensitivity to the material surroundings, but to a heedless and insensitive physical anti-humanism in many aspects of the synthetic environment, in polluted atmosphere, in the destructive contaminations of food and water, in often quite unnecessary artificialities and interferences in the essential human interchanges with the environment. The results on man's body are calamitous, for if industrialism carries with it an obligatory move towards synthesis and the abandonment of nature, man must surely use all his possible wisdom to respect the limits of his physiological being: there are limits that cannot be trespassed without flagrant and terrible punishment in disease.

Far from a negligent attitude to the material things about him, the rise of synthesis should have called into being a greatly added care and circumspection. There are fortunately signs of a re-appraisal of the relationship of man and the physical environment, as in the recent book by Rachel Carson, *Silent Spring*.

So strong has been the assumption of the neutrality of matter that the most elementary questions have barely been asked. Why are material things pleasant or unpleasant? Why are colours, for instance, exhilarating or dull? Why are certain smells pleasant and others repugnant? One can be quite sure, in view of the economies of evolution, that such sensibilities would not have come into being on their own. They have all served some essential human need, which can but mean that in some way they still have to be met.

The reason why colours are so enormously pleasant has already been suggested; they were part of man's creative environment and have been the most potent stimulants of the humanizing emotions. So no doubt have scents, closely associated with flowers. Nasty smells are invariably dehumanizing smells.

Humanizing sounds have not necessarily only been in the form of the human voice. In the environment of nature, there is a perpetual sound-background, in the movements of wind and weather, of rain and water, of birds and cicadas and even of growing things, present the whole time but not consciously realized. Yet, in subtle ways, such sounds may well act as a stimulus, emotional, even physiological. Certainly, if a human being is put into a completely still environment, he develops emotional disturbances rapidly.

All that is in nature and in man can be transcended, into new uses, new elaborations. If this were not possible, man could have created nothing, for the flint is an extension and a true transcendence of his bare nails, and the musical instrument is a transcendence of his voice. It would be surprising if this background of natural sound could not also be used for new purposes, in new ways. No one would suggest that the cacophony of noise in the disorderly urban and industrial milieu today is anything but noise, but the possibility of transcending it is surely there. And not all of it is disturbing even as it is. People get used to their noises of work and living, and miss them when they cease. The noises of moving people, of traffic, of machines, instead of being 'wild' as at present, could be incorporated into an overall environmental concept.

So it is with the shapes and textures of things, changes and alterations, particularly of light and darkness. These may well be natural necessities, that the most artificial of civilizations can never do without. The field of study and experiment is wide open and barely explored. For instance, lighting today is primitive if one compares the bulb or the strip of light to the sheets and wide surfaces of light for which the human eye has been designed. In fact, if such wide stretches of lighting fortify the eyes in contracting the pupils and ensuring a proper irrigation and pressure in the anterior chambers of the eyes, the bulb is about the most irritating and congestive form of lighting it is possible to imagine, and a good deal of the fatigues and visual exhaustions and tensions—as well as blindness in the form of common glaucoma—may be traced to this neglect.

Things are moving in the right direction. The visually enriching nature of texture and especially of organized texture-gradations has been studied, and applications to architecture are being tentatively made. Environmental colour is coming in; special spaces are being planned for human circulation in the midst of the city, air pollution is being controlled. There is a chance that we shall become better and more consistent materialists, and not the crude ones we still are, to the detriment of our emotional selves and of our bodies, and art shows clearly this revived material awareness, in a fascination with the material of art itself, in an aesthetic materialism that is behind a wide group of 'matter paintings'.

High consumption and culture

The increasing abundance of goods which an ever-expanding technology is assuring is having a very decided effect on life's values. Cars and television sets, tape recorders and mini-radios, have become the most desired things of life, and human drudgery is in process of being eliminated in house and office aids, and, on still a wider front, in mechanization and ultimately in a total automation. Much less effort and much more enjoyment are in sight.

To the older generation, who have been brought up in an atmosphere of the stimulus of necessity, if not of dire want, and who are still under the restraints of a paternalistic puritanism, this hedonism is condemned, and the many evils of modern living are blamed to it. But it is an observable fact that mass production brings with it an increased weight of desire. If most of this desiring is venal, one cannot live with such complicated and manifold things as washing-machines and cars without becoming aware of the value of knowledge in well-being. All that man creates is in the last analysis an extension of his being, and can but enrich his entire existential experience. A complicated culture automatically eliminates the virginal satisfactions of a sheer gluttony by an ever-increasing diversity of experience and need.

Whatever the arguments for the kind of abstract art that is now coming out, it could never have taken hold at all in a more elemental, bread-level age. It is, besides everything else, a measure of the luxuriance of living, of its expandedness, both physical and emotional.

Education

No doubt a phase of unmitigated hedonism does come at first, as the goods are turned out ever more cheaply and plentifully. If in the phase of bread-and-butter restraint that preceded it, there was very little time for art at all, in the hedonism which succeeds it it is the 'low arts' that are likely to prime, 'pop', and 'quickie' art. But the importance of art in the personal and social life is likely to rise as one moves into the phase of increasing cultural interest, promoted by education, which we are now entering. The kind of mood involved is shown in the growing purchase of paper-backs and the large attendance at art exhibitions, which contradict the progressive and inevitable deterioration of public cultural interest.

It is usually assumed that the rise in education is the result of an imposition by well-meaning educationalists and social planners. The eagerness of people who come under the impacts of industrialism for the first time is proof that this is not entirely so, and older people can still remember the zeal of the working classes, perhaps more marked in Wales and Scotland than elsewhere in the United Kingdom, for education as the badge of a rise in the standard of living. The claim for social justice, the struggle against artificial class segregations, are as instinctive and come from the same emotional depths.

Education is an automatic accompaniment of the emancipation of modern man, and goes with the industrial revolution that has been responsible for this emancipation. Education may be inadequate and incomplete in many respects, but any education opens up the mind and enhances its general receptivity. Comparison with the virginal receptivity of primitive man is pointless, for the complicatedness of modern life, and a necessarily complicated education, does in a true sense prepare the mind for the effort and even for the need of a complex art, for a positive art effort, in fact. The increasing acceptance of 'modern art' is the fruit of this process.

Work and Leisure

In its initial puritanical stages, the industrial revolution encouraged an ethics of hard work and thrift, evident in the asperities of life in Victorian England, and, more recently, in the Soviet Union and now in China. There is yet very much work to be done in the world, heart-breaking poverty and misery still abound and in many localities are even increasing, but it would be misleading not to take good note of a tendency which appears to be inbuilt in the rise of industrial culture, which may not be fully articulate until it is planetary, but which is here and now none the less evident. A reversal in the ethics of work has taken place. Thrift has become an obsolete virtue: people are not prepared to work in order to save for some theoretical future enjoyment, still less for others, a lost patriarchal virtue; even the stimulus of additional money will not bring out additional effort: people want more leisure and less work, and it is one of the most fortunate provisions of industrialism that this is becoming increasingly possible. More profoundly than one thinks, the spiv is the *avant-garde* of an age when the desirability of work, as a virtue in itself, will have been entirely reversed. One is dealing here with a very ancient human inclination, a natural sloth that goes back to the anthropoids. It is not natural to sweat and slave; it is much more natural to relax and enjoy life, and it is only the stimulation of the ethics of work by a rising industrialism—it would have been impossible without it—that made work appear as the supreme virtue. Mechanization and automation are likely to provide free homes, free health, free food, free travel, in a foreseeable future, with an ever-increasing time to enjoy the benefits of life.

Work as a virtue is characteristically modern-European. In the Middle Ages regular work was performed on no more than half the days of the year, a guarding against work which was ensured by numerous religious and secular holidays. In other cultures, and among all primitives, work is never looked upon as good, but at the most as a necessity. It is more than probable that the strength of the working-class movements in the nineteenth and earlier twentieth centuries was fed by a puritanical and essentially atypical notion of the goodness and virtue of labour as a human activity in itself, and the eclipse of such movements coincides with its recent discredit in an age of increasing plenty and automation.

Fortunately there is a limit to the attractions of scrabble and easy sex, and boredom can be an avenue to cultural interest, especially if a better guided general education prepares the ground for it. It is no coincidence that art becomes more complex and rich according to the complexity and social articulation of a culture, making possible more leisure, and the privileged classes, who have often had no knowledge of the meaning of work, have been the historical supporters of the arts. This instinctive patronage is likely to increase in the natural order of things as what was once privilege becomes generalized.

An experimental and expandable attitude

Science and technology, as much as business and the spirit of industrial enterprise, are experimental at heart, depending for their progress on a ceaseless system of trial and error, of improvisation, invention and rejection, and there is a close analogy here with organic evolution. So great is the speed of this that new prototypes are superseded even before they reach production stage.

There is a stimulus internal to industrialism in this crescendo of effort and experiment; as long as man depended on natural resources, there was always the threat of exhaustion; now that industrialism has passed into the stage of synthesis, this threat itself becomes a stimulus to new synthesis. The rapidity of this process makes the quest for enduring things, still evident in many industries, appear obsolete and traditionally minded; the ethics now is expendability, in all things, in clothes as in cars, and one might usefully apply the principle to buildings. The quest for fixity and endurance, here as elsewhere, betrays a classical attitude quite out of tune with the entire spirit of industrialism in its present phase.

This can but appear as an appalling waste by all previous criteria, yet wastefulness, as in the evolution of life, becomes one of the main stimulants to progress. This attitude of expendability has passed over to art as well. The idea of an utterly precious and everlasting work of art is obsolete, and betrays an inherent and chronic traditionalism. Durability of method and material is ignored, and preciousness scorned. Art has, in fact, become plentiful and the methods of making it ensure an abundance quite incompatible with traditional method. But art is also called upon to provide the one focus of permanence in a welter of transience. There must be some arts which are made to endure (p. 126).

Specialization

The increasing complexity of industrialism and of science and technology has meant a reversal of a previous cultural advantage— the broad view of things, the eclectic regard are not only out of fashion today but are bound to be superficial, for the sheer volume of knowledge required to reach a satisfactory knowing in any subject today prevents any possibility of an effective eclecticism. Specialization in all fields is an essential of industrial culture.

The ideals of a liberal education, the belief in the humanities as the best of all correctives to the contemporary aberrations, is no longer possible, for there is simply no room for quite opposite interests in any specialised curriculum of education.

The bearing on art is clear; if art is to have an effective role to play in life today, it must be 'art now'. There is simply no room for art history as a general subject, only for entirely related arts.

The trend to specialization is evident within the arts themselves, and in art criticism. A broadminded impartiality is a gone virtue. The effective critic is as committed as the artist to a particular aspect of the enormous field of art. Dalliance, once a potential virtue, has become a sign of superficiality, and if a painter like Picasso could get away with it in a period of great experiment—although time has yet to judge the profundity of much of his output—it is simply no longer possible.

Mass appeals and mass communication

Mass communication has enormously increased the visual awareness of people. It is a thought that if man's colour sense evolved in close contact and exercise with coloured things in nature (p. 7), man is now providing a far greater abundance and variety of coloured things than in the most prolific natural environment, and since the human colour sense is physiologically and emotionally still very plastic, a rapid evolution in sensibility may well be taking place. Colour printing, coloured materials and plastics of every kind, and now colour television are bound to call for arts with greater visual articulation.

'Pop' art today is no doubt the successor of peasant art, and attempts to put it over as more can but mislead. 'Meat and two veg' does not exclude Cordon Bleu cooking, and the trivial *divertimenti* of the time did not prevent Mozart from creating great enduring music. There is always an 'easy art' and a 'higher art' demanding more effort and greater sensibility, and if education can go a considerable way to spreading out the latter, there is likely always to be the two. But to assume that a mass culture is bound to work for a permanent debasement of all art is to ignore an enriching, and more-demanding mechanism inbuilt in industrial society that is bound to make 'pop' transitory if always there, ephemeral and light-hearted, while other kinds of art tackle the more penetrative reactions of human beings to the times.

The promotion of youth

Whereas the number of old people is still increasing, there has been a progressive lowering of the age of the managerial groups, a matter of selective survival as the strains and demands of life increase.

Everyone is aware of fundamental changes in attitude during the course of one's life; a society with youth in control is likely to be dynamic and eager for change and innovation, hostile to anchorage, paganly emotional and aesthetically uncluttered. If 'high art' is likely to be somewhat suspect in any excess, so 'pop' is likely to be as ephemeral as the top twenty, possibly not a bad corrective either way.

But in art today, the young are probably given more due and attention than is salutary. Romanticism has not only minimized the need for a tenacity and continuity of struggle necessary to reach any explicit order in art, but it has unfortunately encouraged the view that genius only comes with the flash of youth. The licence given to the young today in painting ensures an ebullience and brash cropping, but much of it is bound to be ephemeral, and opportunism and catch-as-catch-can attitudes that can but bring out light stuff. Only maturity can produce the highly structured and embattled drama of great art.

The break with nature

If one considers the role that nature has played in human creation, in providing human beings with all their characteristics, and, most important, in the relationship of nature and human emotionalism, one will readily realize the extent of the malaise that has followed the break with nature, and the frantic and often pathetic attempts to reintroduce and retain vestiges of a mutilated nature in the midst of urban life.

But to be effective emotionally, nature must be natural. Besides being seen as alive, beautiful, harmonious, invigorating, it must be seen as pure and unblemished. It is especially this quality that is absent in what is left of nature in industrial conditions. This quality of unblemish, of purity, is a very necessary emotional stimulus; without it, nature ceases to be natural; it is indispensable for the humanizing emotions, for a certain purity of response, as much as selflessness and self-control in behaviour, have been essential virtues from the start of the human race; effective parental cooperation in human breeding would have been impossible without it, and here purity does stand for something opposite to animal sexual promiscuity (p. 3). And so to see nature as pure, as elevating, as emotionally quickening and sanctifying, as harmonious and noble, is a deep human requirement. As soon as nature becomes visibly impure, contaminated, spoilt, then it is rejected entirely from the emotional depths.

Whatever the Romantics say, and the nature conservancy supporters maintain, nature is largely already dead in the hearts of modern human beings, which is why they often treat it so badly and negligently. And it is this that has made artists seek an enhancement of nature in art, as in Impressionism, and when that has finally failed, in an art which dispenses with nature altogether.

For all art has a symbolic purity. There is no such thing as an impure art, in the sense of an overall vicious, licentious, cruel, pornographic appeal. Eroticisms and aggressions are invariably redeemed by the humanizing attributes of art, by harmonies of form and structure and line, overall integration, by colour, and so even the most depraved subjects can come to have a humanizing appeal in art, as in Goya's 'Horrors of War' or in Picasso's 'Guernica'.

Up to the time of the Romantics, the rising industrial revolution had left considerable areas even in England untouched, and the privileged classes, who largely promoted the Romantic Movement in spite of its later turn into an idealistic socialism in Morris, could afford to indulge in a delightful escapism, in lavish parks and elaborate gardens of delight. But today, all such possibilities have gone. The denaturing of what is left of nature can but proceed to an ultimate and total denaturing. Even now, the ancient function of trees of converting carbon dioxide back into oxygen is failing, and the increasing production of carbon dioxide by industry is forming a blanket of insulation around the world which, unless corrected, is bound to lead to an increase in world temperature, with a faster melting of glaciers and far-reaching consequences. Plans are ready for the replacement of this ancient function of trees by air-regenerating units, which in time will be spread over the face of the earth much like the water towers of today.

As the city in time comes to provide in man-made form all human requirements, physical and emotional, the city parks and gardens will go; the pleasure they still afford is proof of the failure of the city in its present form. Nucleated and intercommunicating, like some elaborate Martian map, the spaces between the cities and industrial areas will be largely neutral, emotionally meaningless and practically without function, for agriculture itself will have been replaced by far more efficient systems of food production, probably in good part in the oceans.

This inevitable vision appears horrific only to the romantically biased view that man should never attempt to replace nature, and that any attempts at replacement are bound to be inferior if not actually harmful. The evil of a nostalgic regard for nature, and its pathetic symbolization in the city window-box and back garden, and its most monstrous recent perversion, itself the sure sign of the death of nature in our hearts, the artificial flower, is that proper attempts to grapple with the enormous problems of making the city and the urban way of life more human and humanizing are not forthcoming. The sooner industrial human beings can face the fact in full that here and now nature is done with, the sooner will man's synthetic environment become congenial to a full, happy, and healthy life.

The price and promise of artificiality

The price we are paying for this interim period of maladjustment is severe, widespread frustration and frequent outbursts into aggression and antihumanisms of one terrible kind or another, accompanied by an emotional desensitization which was especially evident in the earlier, more chaotic spread of industrialism, the choking down of human feeling in a world grown hostile and dark to it, in the dour puritanism of the Black Country and of the Ruhr, in a rodent feeling of social injustice and inferiority hostile to art in any form. The only kind of imagery tolerable under such dehumanizing conditions is that of a dead, gone age, which makes no emotional claims. If the soul is a corpse, it is best left covered, and when taste is at all displayed, it tends to be atrocious and hideous.

Neurosis, always a result of ineffective emotional adaptation to life, is common to all industrial civilization. Although it accounts for much individual misery, it does also unleash a considerable amount of energy and drive, the reactive restlessness so typical of the trapped animal, and it is this that undoubtedly fuels the amazing enterprise of all industrial communities. One sees it in every aspect of city and industrial living, in the rush, in a love of speed and excitement, in so many forms of energetic expression. With a dangerous, hysterical, and aggressive streak to it, none the less industrialism generates in this way its own momentum to further endeavour, a remarkable inbuilt mechanism for self-perpetuating expansion which is showing every sign of taking mankind beyond his planetary limitation.

This drive and exuberance can be seen in all artificializing cultures, and seems to be all the keener as the culture moves away from nature. It arises also when nature turns against man, in the restlessness of migrations and the amazing feats of ice-age peoples and nomads. All that industrialism has done is to tap into this old reactive restlessness and strike upon a *furor* of agitation and drive never known before, a degree of agitation that makes the modern industrial human being in this feature alone quite different from any other cultural product and not to be compared at all with the primitive. A good deal of this has gone to destructive and fiendish ends, and it may yet spell the end of man on earth, but this seems to be the risk and the price one has to pay for the fantastic dynamism of industrial civilization, its most characteristic feature, and one must expect that its most characteristic art is likely to be some frantic expression of energy.

But bearing in mind the dialectics of human nature, one must expect that such an agitation is bound to call for a condition the very opposite of it in some form of contemporary quietism. Such revived interests as Zen, and in the less elevated form of tranquillizers and the libidinal exhaustions of a physical sexuality, are a part of this reaction. In painting, one finds a variety of 'cool', esoteric, 'soft' imageries, a kind of stepback and disengagement, a respite and revival from the throb and bustle rather than a turning of one's back to it. The call of the beat remains the most

typical and desired reaction, and the kind of removal and meditation practised in the past is now meaningless and quite impossible.
The balance of the energetic today is 'cool', still active, never
resignation and retreat. Traditional Japanese culture had made a
particular study of the intricacies of civilized living, and had
discovered practices compatible with it that we have yet to
discover and apply, which may account for the Japanese successes
in industrial living today.

The decline of idealism and romanticism

Idealism is in disrepute, and in a pragmatic age appears as a subtle
form of escapism if not an open pathology of feeling. Let anyone
who would defend idealism trace the course of it in Germany, in
its increasing references to death and pain, in poets like Schiller,
and in its monstrous perversions in Hitler. It is no coincidence that
Hitler enjoyed Wagner, for Wagner's scramblings of melody and
his languorous and sickly erotic idealism both belong to that
tragic period of the break with nature of the rising industrial age.
Idealism, like naturalism in art, is the reaction to a threatened
break with nature and a snapping of the most ancient emotional
fountains, the source of all pristine human enjoyment, and if it
was at first an enhancement of the beauties and harmonies of a
naturalistic intercourse, it later became fiendishly pathological.
If there cannot be love, then there shall be death, and the history
of Europe from the closing nineteenth century is one ghastly
illustration of this Freudian prophecy.

In ordinary life, romanticism is roughly speaking senti-
mentalism. People today, particularly the young, have no time for
this, are matter of fact; not idealistic but existentially minded.
A practical attention to living problems is, in fact, incompatible
with romanticism and idealism, which can prosper only under
conditions of relative unreality and social introversion, elements
now quite evident in Fascism.

Although distantly related with what most people mean by
'romantic', the Romantic Movement has had an enormous influence on the history of the modern art movements. It is particularly English, in that the historical and physical isolation of
England from the Continent enabled it to maintain for longer and
with much less corruption an idealistic romanticism. It is still a big

influence in England, which accounts for a good deal of the lack of connexion of English painting today with happenings else-where. Historically, this movement, especially active in poetry, expresses the reaction from the depths at the threats against nature, at its denaturings. Since a nature-tied emotionalism is deeply humanizing—that was its original intention—the Romantic's view of nature and of man is delicate, humanistic, aesthetically sensitive, and against the rising inhumanisms and brutalities and crudities of industrial living. It is not only for nature and at heart against in-dustry, but also against science and the progressive spirit of the age.

The Romantic artist's attitude to nature must be understood. He develops his 'vision' through an imaginative exchange with nature, is stimulated by beauty and by a kind of mystical inter-course, aspires to its nobility and purity.[53] 'Inspiration' comes as a more or less sudden climax in this intercourse—the symbolic recapitulation of the sexual pattern is significant—the entire process is barely subliminal, a kind of daydreaming, a symbolic living *through* appearances. It is the contamination of nature by industrialism and a growing urbanism that made this kind of intercourse no longer possible—it would have meant that the Romantic would have had to embrace a corrupt woman, and it is today no longer possible at all. Nature has become a diseased whore. Romanticism survives as a purely intellectual nostalgia, and the words 'vision' and 'inspiration' have quite lost their meaning to artists.

But if Romanticism has no bearing on the arts of today, and is, in fact, against them in act and spirit, one must concede that as a movement, it was the first to call for a greater degree of freedom from traditional servitudes. In its free lyrical interplay with nature, it was in its time against traditional disciplines and against a sub-servient realism; reality had to be beautified, ennobled, purified, and there can be no doubt that the English contribution to the rise of the Impressionists is not only in a very few painters, especially Turner, but in a far more pervasive literary, poetical, and even social attitude to liberalism in the arts.

Relativism in living

In the past, people have been governed by avowed standards, references, and objectives in all fields; even if they did not abide by them, the standards were there none the less, and the best possible human condition was looked upon as one of utmost orderliness, an evident application of determinism and of the classical outlook. The objectives and references were invariably idealistic, and echo the most ancient human aspirations to goodness, beauty, order, unity, self-sacrifice, duty, and communal effort, the field of the 'humanizing emotions', themselves so closely related to nature. The eclipse of nature, the decline of idealism and the reversal of a rigid determinism in all fields of thought and feeling mean that relativism has passed over into common life. Rigid theoretical standards in trade and profession as much as in ethics or religion are out, and instead, the criterion of justifiable action is pragmatic and relativistic.

Although deplored in many quarters, this is a fact and a most important feature of modern living, and so strong is it that one can but wonder if it has not been the premise of relativism in science and philosophy, rather than the other way round. It is a fact that ideas in science only mature when some sort of emotional preparation has been going on. No evidence against determinism, for instance, would have made indeterminism acceptable at the height of the nineteenth century. The fact is that life as well as science and thought have become relativistic, and art discernibly so. It has slipped out of the hands of the traditional art historians and become an 'open' subject. Artists can become accepted professionals without any academic training, and literally any approach to art is possible.

The end of finalism

With the general relativism of modern times has come the rejection of a belief in attainable ends and final targets. There is, in fact, no longer an 'end in itself' in any current process or activity. Every mechanical development and industrial enterprise opens up an ever-increasing plurality of potential lines of endeavour. Machines themselves are becoming so complex that they offer, like living things, opportunities and suggestions beyond their original intention. This crescendo of development makes any thinking in terms of definite ends impermissible, and a quite new continuity-thinking is coming in, in industry, commerce, and science, and this can but have a repercussion in all human fields, including sociology, politics, and philosophy. The artist has, in fact, been one of the first to give up endthinking and feeling.

Changed sex patterns

Unquestionably the most important accompaniment of the break with nature is in changed sexual behaviour. All culture and civilization entail some degree of disturbance in the genetic patterns of an emotionalized sexuality, and every culture reacts in its own ways to the inevitable disturbances and human threats which such an interruption entails. In the most artificializing of all civilizations, our reactions are bound to be particular and special.

The importance of sex should need no emphasis; it is not only the means of species continuity, but in human beings, of even greater importance, it has become the means of a progressive humanization within the individual and within society, so that one can pertinently say that in the case of man, and uniquely in his case, sex has passed beyond a direct procreative activity to become the means of maintaining and furthering the characteristics of humanity during the entire course of an individual life in all human societies. The importance of this conclusion must be stressed; for it means that no longer can sex be looked upon as purely and entirely 'sexual' in the case of man.

Because of this, one must be very careful to keep in mind the essential, unique features of human sexuality, and not indulge in generalizations about animal sexuality or confuse the innumerable existential modifications with the genetic pattern. Except among the relatively few animals in which prolonged parental co-operation became essential for survival, the normal animal pattern is maximal fertilization, which in human language means a maximum promiscuity. Wherever this primordial and general promiscuity has had to be reversed emotionalism has been the usual way of doing it. But among animals, emotionalism is not used in the same way as in the human species.

All the human traits that distinguish man from the animal—love, kindness, affection, care for others, and selflessness, a sense of duty and obligation, co-operation and communal feeling, the appreciation of beauty, nobility, harmony and purity—come from the emotionalism special to human sex, and there can be no doubt that the focus of this emotionalism from the start of human creation has been the family group. It was this special group that separated man from the other anthropoids, among which degrees of a sexual free-for-all still prevail. Although biological thinkers in the last century were inclined to imagine the primitive human condition as one of promiscuity, anarchy, and bestiality, the evidence against this is now considerable, from the study of primitives and from psychology.

The family group is, however, by no means a closed, fixed group. It varies enormously in its constitution, from a strict monogamy, to polyandry, polygamy, and large, more diffuse groupings involving several generations and extramarital inclusions. But since the biological intention of the family is to provide proper nurturing for the defenceless and growing human infant, who requires it over a number of years, to leave as much brain time as possible open for learning, the trend is towards enduring unions of one man and one woman, and this basic pattern is only modified provided the procreative duties are respected. If sexual freedom is allowed, as it is, for instance, among the Polynesians, then there must be compensating social adjustments, such that children are accepted in the family irrespective of paternity.

In any examination of human sex on a world basis one cannot help coming to the conclusion that if there is a specific, basic type in some form of enduring monogamy, human sex is exceedingly plastic and adaptable by nature, as indeed it would have to be if man was to survive as a communal creature under the most varied conditions of life.

In looking at sexual behaviour today one must bear this in mind, for it is too easy, with a strong puritanical past still so close, to dogmatize and look for lasting codes and fixed standards. There need be none, provided the human and the humanizing requirements are met—that is the essential criterion—and one can start confidently from the premise that if industrial living has dramatically shattered patterns of previously established sexual behaviour, then there is every chance that human beings will be able to elaborate new ones in better league with present-day conditions.

We find ourselves in an alarming period of transition, when the old patterns are visibly breaking up, and the new ones are not yet properly formed. Until they are formed, there is bound to be maladjustment, even chaos. With urbanization, and the diversification of social life, the family is attacked from almost every angle. Children are encouraged to develop new loyalties in the course of education, the ancient loyalties and servitudes between family members are no longer possible, and the inevitable frustrations and irritations of an artificial life can but demand freer sexual outlets. As a result, an ever-increasing number of children grow up without the former nurturing influences, the emotionalizing influence of the mother, the controlling influence of the father, roles probably as ancient as mankind. A degree of insensitivity and a callous, dehumanized outlook among the young is inevitable, with its all too evident outlets in social aggression and crime.

If the old sex order is collapsing and cannot be revived, new patterns of order will certainly have to be found. They are, in fact, arising almost imperceptibly among the people now, even if superficially a stake is still held in the old conventions and practices. Here and now, the practice of sex is being separated from the function of reproduction. This is likely to go all the way till breeding ceases to be the more or less accidental thing it is at present and is undertaken by professional breeders, selected and subsidized. The still numerous bourgeoisie will smile smugly at this suggestion while they go about their ancestral breeding habits, but the trends are against them, and if the new arrival in former times brought congratulations, the time of reprimand is at hand.

When this trend is more articulate, the advantages are likely to be enormous: not only will people be able to indulge in the freedom which the pressure of events has made expedient, but for the first time in human history the same skill and selection will go into human breeding as has long gone into the breeding of domestic animals. With an increase in genetic damage through radioactive fall-out and injurious chemicals in food and air, this is likely to synchronise with a genetical imperative. Within a few generations, some of the most ravaging ills could be entirely eliminated—even cancer is coming to be genetically suspect—while people can avoid the demoralizing and humiliating curettings and abortions now current, in which the imminent promise of a simple system of contraception will prove handy. As it is, a fifth of the births in some great industrial cities are illegitimate, and the amount of abortion that goes on in all industrial societies is ever on the increase. Not to face this fact, and the underlying change and trend that it reveals, is sheer moral dishonesty. One of the first things that will have to go, the last survival of an age of patriarchal values, is the paternal prerogative, and the reversion to an ancient system whereby it is the creative agent, the mother, who decides the child's status and name, a system already accepted in Sweden.

But the emergence of a quite new sexual structure does not mean a condoning of promiscuity. If sex is innately plastic and adaptable to social conditions, and if a fair measure of freedom is tolerable, the human emotional make-up is quite incompatible with promiscuity. Sexual opportunism invariably leads to an animalizing of sex and a desensitization of the roots of all human feeling. Interhuman loyalty and mutual consideration, not only materially but above all emotionally, is, in fact, the only way of being human, and one does always find some traces of it, even in the most depraved circumstances. In the 'milieu', in the gangster-doms of Sicily and Chicago, in the teddy and youth gangs of the malignant cities of today, one comes upon contorted roots of loyalties, which, in more humanizing conditions, would surely have found fuller human expression. It is more than likely that an emergent sexual ethics will restore the value and dignity of enduring sexual unions, but in freedom and without the primitive obligations that survive at present. The failure of a partial step in these directions in the earlier years of the Russian revolution does not point to the wrongness or impossibility of it, only to prematurity and miscarriage and a return of traditional moralities. But if progress is never straight, the long-term trend is clear enough even now.

Civilization has also profound effects on both the intensity and the ways in which sex is expressed. All too often, these changes are looked upon as degenerative and regressive, but they are not necessarily so. A more androgynous outlook seems to go with cultural refinement and sensitivity, as primitive demarcations become more blurred, and in our own times this has taken the form of both a visual levelling and an emotional one.[54] It is not only that since the suffragettes women have desired all the advantages formerly reserved to men, but they often dress in ways more masculine, and enjoy their sex in ways which are noticeably masculine and would have been quite foreign to women in previous ages.[55] A comparable feminization process has occurred among men, and if some of this tendency is bound to go into active homosexual practices, there has been a noticeable softening up of men's clothing and an attenuation of masculine features in general, and sensitivity, greater refinement, artistic and other cultural interests are a part of this change.

It is a fact that creative artists have a marked bisexual constitution, even if they happen to remain heterosexual, for as Freud pointed out in his study of Dostoevesky, a homosexual predisposition in some form is part of the creative neurosis. This being so, a severe either/or attitude to sex is becoming obsolete and appears to belong to a more primitive emotional stage. Androgynous reactions appear to be an essential part of a higher cultural reaction, and many of the highest achievements of culture in all fields have come from what one might call an androgynous ambiguity, the move from a primitive monovalence to a more elaborate emotional polyvalence which is implicit in ancient magical thought and in alchemy.[56] Although this observation can in no way condone bestial and degrading practice, the trend to an emotional androgyny can be seen as an evolutive, not as a degenerate one, the innate drive within every human being towards emotional completion and fulfilment, and the natural tendency for this to become at least in part realized within one person and one sex as the level of emotional refinement and range increases.

Neurosis itself is tied up with the sexual confrontation, and the result of failure, not so much of finding physical satisfaction, as the emotional fulfilment and promise innate in all sexual drives. Any culture, any civilization is bound to interfere to some extent in this, and so to spur towards some degree of emotional transcendence, some displacement of the emotional libidinal energies, often stimulating them ferociously in the process. So that if one finds neurosis in great increase, also one finds the energy and upgrading emotional drives behind all civilization and cultural development.

It is significant that such inherently socializing forces as one finds in Buddhism, in Hinduism, in Mithraism, in Taoism, in Judaism and Christianity and in Islam and the recent social preoccupations of Marxism have appeared in the disturbed and anguished womb of the most complex cultures. It seems to be a deeply insown tendency, one might almost say a provision, that the rise of the level of social organization brings out a promise contained in the primeval bisexual love of man and woman for passage into a universalizing love of all one's fellow creatures.

As society has moved from its more primitive and localized forms into ever more expansive ones, so art has passed on from the primitive supplying of totems and the marks of sectarianism to more socializing services, of caste and class and religion, of entire communities. In doing this, art has itself moved on from a more primitive emotional range of appeal to the more universal.

From its sexual origins, the emotionalism behind sex is evidently of two polarities, 'male' and 'female', and primitive art is often more clearly marked as one or the other, not only figuratively, but in such attributes as essentially masculine force, energy, structure, and the more feminine expressiveness and loose emotion, the more tender and receptive. These opposites become blended in the arts of higher cultures, and so art reflects the move towards an androgynous emotionalism. Ever more women are artists, a former male prerogative. In this respect, it should be noted that if the physical demarcations of the sexes are clear enough—though one cannot overstress the physiological overlaps in everyone—the 'male' and 'female' emotional complements are far less fixed, and, being emotional, this is just what one would expect. Within every person, an emotional androgyny exists as a most ancient and deeply human feature, and it is this fact no doubt that accounts for its eruption as soon as refining civilization and culture allow it to be actualized, in art, in life, in outlook, for it is the actualization of a fundamental and essential premise of humanization, the move beyond the barriers of primitive appeal.

Today, the city reflects the human sex dilemma and crisis; the old order survives within it, in its forms and functions, while the new possibilities of the city as the ideal locus of human life in an age ever more synthetic have yet to be realized, a situation of a schizoid and pathological nature.[57] In some very involved way, perhaps the problem will only be solved when mankind shall have worked out its emotional ones, especially in a new and more effective sexual structure. The two are intimately related, environment and sex, for from the start they have worked together towards the humanization of man, and if man is to find the ways of humanizing his new synthetic environment, he may well first of all have to find ways and means of sexual and emotional behaviour compatible and consistent with a truly human disposition.

Changes in society

Politically minded writers have tended to ascribe the social revolution of our times to the ideas and political agitations of certain personalities. Yet the main social changes that have taken place in the past 150 years can be directly related to the industrial revolution.

For the older people who have lived through the intense political fevers of the earlier century, themselves the consequence of the bitter struggles of the preceding centuries, to minimize the importance of political action appears as an affront, yet when history is written with a more detached view, the social alterations are likely to be seen to follow on the progressive alterations and upheavals of industrialism. At first, the direct influence was the primitive mercantile capitalism that came from the Renaissance, and beyond it, much farther back to the trading cultures of the Mediterranean. A more socially conscious capitalism succeeded it as the machine itself enabled the slavery of brawn to be relieved, and socialism came with the need to share out the harvest of a rising industrialism. But from now on we are at the end of the isms. Industry and technology become the direct means of meeting all possible human need; agitation and intervention, political, idealistic, are no longer necessary.

Coincident with this remarkable event, not at all foreseen by the political theorists of the last century, there have been profound social changes. The so-called working classes have come to enjoy the benefits that formerly only went with privilege, and so in one stroke the main stimulus to political interest and action has been removed by industrialism in its growing impetus of cornucopic supply. If in the early phases of the industrial revolution, the organization and management went to the bourgeoisie, and if they were in time succeeded by a more distinct managerial class, today there is a growing intrusion of the technologist into the decisive ranks of management and organization. It is ever less acumen and ability in practical matters that counts than know-how.

The situation which is now arising can be clearly predicted: a large preponderance of well-fed, well-housed people, abundantly provided for, and a rising *élite* of a new technocracy. In the long run, these are likely to be the two main social distinctions. An entirely classless society is as mythical as a take over by the 'masses'. People are much happier provided for than agitating, and much prefer to have all the things of life done for them than to have to bother with any of the doing themselves.

The only possibility of intercommunal struggle would be if the *élite* should abuse its powers and oppress the majority. This is most unlikely for practical as well as personality considerations. Practically, there will no longer be any need for exploitation and oppression; there will be more than enough to go round, and an ever-increasing amount of it. Men have not been slave-drivers by choice, and slavery as a system was abandoned as soon as new sources of energy became available—as no doubt it would return if industrialism collapsed in a nuclear war.

And with the new technocrats, the old tests of competitive ruthlessness, still at work in liberal capitalistic society, will be largely superseded by the competitiveness of knowledge and efficiency, a machinery of survival and selection already well under way, and such a selection, being educational and intellectual, will work on an altogether higher plane. Certain qualities of toughness and drive will be as necessary as before, but there will be room for ramifying intellectual, artistic, and humanistic sympathies. But even more decisive, it will be an 'open' classless *élite*, to which anyone, with the talents and qualifications, can aspire, and the main source of an ancient social gnawing—the inheritance of any form of material privilege—will have been eliminated.

Just as the 'class struggle' is coming to an end, so the days of politics and of politicians are closing. They are not likely to accept this quietly, but the force of industrial progress is against them. One can say with a fair optimism that this trend is likely to pass from the national to the international, and the structure of human society to approach progressively further to an international, pan-planetary society. As it is, the rising technological *élite* is operating internationally; the big companies have ramifications all over the world; the Common Market, the work of specialists, not of politicians, has had, in fact, to struggle against their persistent interferences and sabotage. An international meeting of scientists in 1958 in Switzerland would have ended in agreement in nuclear matters had it not been for the intervention of politicians and curt orders for the scientists to return home.

At present this rising *élite* is neither fully aware of its powers nor of its human duties. Many of the technologists today come from lower income backgrounds, and still suffer from various forms of psychological inferiority and their attitude to such questions as art are myopic. But this is likely to be remedied as the ancient class barriers break down and recruitment is on a more effective communal and educational basis, and, above all, as education itself becomes truly equitable and communal.

As every psychologist knows, leisure is attended by an increase in introspection, and that is the first step to individuation. Only in a society anaesthetized by intense communal effort, as in the post-revolutionary days of France, of Russia, and today in China, can the natural trend towards greater degrees of individual expression and freedom be temporarily reversed by mass reactions. It has been one of the greatest fallacies of social thinkers to assume that collectivization and deindividualization were inevitable.

But this development of individualism can but be within a social framework, which is bound to become more articulate and decisive in all human matters as the populations of the world rise to planetary saturation, a state which is a long way off, for with proper reforms in food habits—the present 'mixed' dietaries entail an enormous waste of land—with ocean farming and new methods of food production, the population of the planet is likely to exceed greatly the present forecasts.

The romantic, always fearful of threats against his isolation and in defence of his back garden, sees this as nothing but degradation. Yet with nature gone, human beings themselves become the most potent and vitalizing influence one upon another, and the beneficial effects of a communally directed psychiatry are proof of the integrating and whole-making powers of human beings upon one another. If human density is at present often frustrating, the fault lies with the architect, in the city as it is today. Organized congestion is likely to prove the highest state of human living.

Conclusions

On every cultural front there are the signs of a revolt against the ideology and world view of the Renaissance, of its associations with classicism, a combination which has continued with modifications until the close of the nineteenth century in growing force and dominion, and still survives in decline to this day. In the course of this revolt, European man is questioning his view and attitudes to all the fundamental criteria of existence, of thought and feeling, attitudes to space, to time, to matter, to the organization of human life, to science and to art.

Matter, so long looked upon as dead, is pregnant again with miracle, and since a sacred view of life can only come from a sacred view of matter and of all the creatures and states that arise from it, there are the growing possibilities of a new definition of humanism, of man's place in the Universe, of the importance and dignity of the human presence.

Every aspect of the modern age proves that man is pre-eminently a creative creature, the most remarkable aspect of that creativeness that runs right through the cosmos. Nothing occurs without some element of wonder in it. A modern car is something more than a useful machine, a well-designed pen becomes a loved object, and the lights of a city can be more wondrous and magical than any pagan sunset.

That we are in a world of flux and becoming has penetrated into common literature. The explorations of psychology are in every play. The cultural transformation is not only affecting scientists and artists, but is visibly occurring in the midst of everyday living, in every human spirit. Admittedly, a culture lives on many levels, and as yet, only a few are consciously aware of these alterations, of the new reactions from the depths and the heights, of the dramatically altered world itself. Perhaps the overriding value of the new imageries in painting is that they make this evident, in their clash with the imageries of the past, in their startling evidence of revolution. They have much more to do, but this is a necessary labour also.

But when all this has been said, it would be ludicrous to suggest that European man is only the product of the industrial revolution. Indeed, the way he has reacted and so produced this revolution is the product of his past, pragmatic, materialistic, adventurous, and immensely courageous. But with these practical qualities that have made the revolution possible here and nowhere else, at this time and at no other, are qualities which are also not materialistic and which have a great bearing on art. From the remotest past, the European has had a strong dramatic sense, in the theatre of ancient Greece, in the Bible, and still very active today, a vague realization of man's pathetic cosmic position and the response of courage and resolve in spite of it, there in Lear, as in Camus. Materialism itself carries something of this stand, a majestic defiance of the gods, and Existentialism comes to extol man's confrontation with the void of a chronic incapacity to 'know' the Universe as reason has mistakenly made him believe in the past that he could come to know it.

One can face this dramatic sensibility, or escape from it; one can play the fool in the light of man's perpetual quandary and glide over the need for a desperate and ultimately hopeless heroics, or one can savour it in all the labouring greatness that man can aspire to, of the mind, of the body. One finds both in Shakespeare, and most people oscillate between the one and the other in the course of their lives. Only few, and then but rarely, can stand up to the dramatic moment. In times of great confusion, there can be no doubt that by far the most common reaction is the reaction of the clown, the antics of *homo ludens*, the glorious tragic buffoon. In an age like ours, so dramatic in itself, faced with the risks of imminent and total devastation, the urge to laugh and be merry is all the greater. The demands of great art become something of a bore. But great art is still there, as ever dramatic, the one quality that distinguishes it from the art of fools.

Comedy is the dialectic of tragedy, that quality of an aroused and merciful compassion for human vanity and failure, for the follies and vices of life, which one finds in Cervantes, Dickens, Molière, Aristophanes, and which is quite different from humour. As Freud pointed out, the joke is usually a catharsis for baser passions; comedy can be great art, and is quite different from the art of fools.

But if it would be wrong to belittle the preparatory and formative past, the congenital baggage that each one of us still carries with the echoes of battles and burning crosses, it is desperately necessary to jettison what is now obsolete and to pay entire attention to the challenge of the new. We can begin with this ruthless sifting in art itself. As we have already said, the bulk of what is now going around as 'modern' is nothing but the traditional served up in new dress. Yet, revolutionary as the present is, and wrong as it undoubtedly is to look back and hope to find leads into the present from a radically different past, there is one aspect of art that must be looked at more closely and historically before proceeding to the really valid art of our times, and that is technique.

There is an analogy in science. Although there are no bridge-heads between the old and the new physics in concepts, in principles, the new physics has, in fact, come from the perfection of techniques and methods which were worked out in the old science. If there is no continuity of principles, in that quite new worlds can suddenly come to view, there can be a continuity in the methods of exploration, in the methods of labour, in the kinds of human skill.

6

THE VALID IMAGE

The importance of technique

THERE are two dissimilar approaches to art: what one can 'see' in it, and how it is made.

For most people, including art historians, it is what one can read into art that matters, and it is probably true that the greatness of any art is decided by its elasticity in this matter. That this can vary greatly even in traditional realist art, the long dusty shelves of contradictory art writing are there to prove. The appreciation of art is in truth at all times a creative projection on the part of the beholder, an emotional exercise which can but vary with different people and alter in the same person. There may well be some accord between what the artist himself can see in his work, and what another sees in it, and this must to some considerable extent be the case if they are both truly contemporary, but all aesthetic experience is individually recreative.

It is a fact which often seems strange to people not directly concerned with the making of art that artists themselves are far more concerned with the practical, technical things of art, and that their discussions and interest in the art of others centres around this. It is not that artists are unconcerned with the social and philosophical implications of their work, but they are in no better position than anyone else in this respect. But their technical pronouncements and pursuits are always of immense importance.

The artist's interest in technique is so primary and overriding that it usually cuts out the kind of art appreciation that goes on in others. If he is drawn to another artist's work, it is for the technique of it; the emotional impact and extensions seldom claim him. So much so that if one sees a person greatly emotionally aroused about the work of another, he is unlikely to be an artist.

But this does not imply that an artist's attitude to technique is mechanical or superficial. The artist has to struggle to find the right imageries, by exhausting trial and error, by continual rejection and destruction, and if this process quietens down in quiet times, it becomes anguishing in times of change, requiring new expression to altered reactions. Then all the canons of previous art become useless, all must be begun again.

Under such conditions, the artist is ceaselessly experimental. If he comes in time to find one particular set of techniques that produces the right kind of image for him, in the course of it he dabbles with all sorts of variants and adventures which are laid aside on the way. At the time, these are discarded and ignored, for they do not meet the requirements. But if conditions change again, a future generation of artists can find these shelved discoveries of great use. It is a fact of great interest that a painting popular because of other appeals can contain these technical discards, which are not noticed at the time, but which become very obvious to succeeding generations of artists who come to need them; the work of the Impressionists abounds in such relics, as in the occasional extraordinary freedoms in brushwork of even the most traditional masters.

In the rise of the 'Traditional Moderns', one finds a great technical anxiousness among artists, and they look about, at the past, at each other; many artists go through virtually identical periods as in the Cubist Legers, Braques, and Picassos. Many of these painters avow an interest in the painters of the past, but it should be recalled that this interest is not in their image so much as in the technique it contains, and often in aspects of it that have been concealed and ignored up to now.

So it has been with the rise of the quite new paintings. If the paintings of the 'Traditional Moderns' have nothing in common with the new paintings as far as their actual imageries are concerned and they are indeed mutually contradictory, there may well be technical suggestions of profit and interest. With the distinction between what one sees in art and the technique of it before one, it will be useful to take a glance at the art which has preceded the present[58] and to see in what ways its technical discoveries have helped the artists of the new painting to find their own ways. It is this technical interest that makes artists visit galleries and exhibitions of paintings apparently quite different as imageries from their own, and in a very true sense, artists go to current advanced exhibitions to see each other's technical display; they are 'artists exhibitions', and it follows that if anyone wants to get a distinct view of art apart from the usual one of 'taking it in', he should come to some understanding of the technical problems involved.

The technical succession

The Traditional Modern can be separated technically into the structural, the modulating, and the intellectual. The last term is particularly unfortunate, but it does cover a group of imageries in which attitudes, thoughts, and theories of art in relation to society have been important.

As far as the structural painters are concerned, one can dismiss their contribution summarily as thoroughly classical and static in spirit, a spirit evident in the neo-classicist period of Picasso, in the Rayonnism of Larionov, in the Constructivism of Gabo and Moholy Nagy, of Mondrian, in the Cubism of Braque, Picasso, Gris, Leger, Marcoussis, in the néo-plasticisme of Van Doesberg, and in the architectural connexions of de Stijl with their present-day supporters and revivers in 'hard edge'. It must, however, be mentioned that Moholy Nagy was also interested in moving imageries and dynamic attitudes that have important outlets today.

Modulation varies from a discreet alteration to the scrambling up one finds in the Impressionists, and many of the big historical names come here, Cézanne—he is also importantly structural—Monet, Seurat, etc. The present-day Abstract Impressionists come directly from them. An important group avoided the scrambling by a more definite attention to sheets of pure colour and form, with the prototype in Gauguin, and if the scrambling modulators have nothing to offer and their emotional ties are too strongly steeped in nature, the paintings of Gauguin, Klee, Kandinsky, Modigliani, Matisse, Chagall, Dufy, Jawlensky, Marc, Macke, members of 'les Fauves' and 'Die Brucker', provide many suggestions of the direct expressive use of colour, foreshadowing the modern Expressionists.

A half-way world also exists between the structural and the modulating painters, proof of the common rooting of both in tradition and in nature. Kandinsky is the key example, his work oscillating between what he called 'improvisations' and 'compositions', also in Feininger, in Metzinger, in the American Macdonald Wright, in Kupka, and in the Orphists—the Delaunays in particular. They are important, in spite of a strong nature association, for at times they do show the suggestions of a breakout of a Euclidean geometry into a geometry of imprecision—softenings by colour and light which are virtually Rothkoesque in parts.

The intellectual artists come with the Surrealists, with Futurism, and Dada, all accompanied by much intellectual flourish and activity. The Surrealism one finds in such painters as Klee, Ernst, de Chirico, Miro, Arp, Baumeister, and the Futurists with Balla, Severini, Boccioni, Carra, Marinetti, and Dada with Duchamp, Schwitters. The 'assemblers' of today, the neo-dada and neo-surrealists, are their direct heirs, perhaps the most important way to independence apart from Expressionism.

The Expressionists find their prototypes and very great technical support from Van Gogh and Munch, and a long continental Germanic and Russian succession in Holder, Ensor, Kirchener, Schmidt-Rottluff, Rouault, Soutine, Permeke. Matthew Smith is an English rarity. Painters like Kokoschka, Soutine, Ensor, and Nolde, often dither in a half-world of modulation and Expressionism. All these, especially 'les Fauves', and perhaps particularly Matisse and Klee, have had their very great technical influence on the valid techniques to today. The Futurists, although thoroughly traditional in their technical approaches, did bring in a certain brashness and dynamism, and the influence of the Surrealists on painters like Pollock is admitted.

This evaluation means that masters like Cézanne, Braque, and Kandinsky have really no significant succession in the new painting; their greatness today comes from the fact that they are the last great manipulators of a thoroughly traditional approach, and it is in such names as Picasso, Matisse, Munch, Klee, Miro, and Schwitters that greater affinities exist.

With this all too brief look into the immediate past, and before moving on to the really valid painting of our times, one cannot overemphasize the distinction to be made between technique and image in this respect. As far as the imagery is concerned, and it is this that interests most people, there are absolutely no bridgeheads between the past and the present.

The time may come when people will be sufficiently detached from the influences of the past to be able to appreciate its arts without the certainty of contaminating their contemporary tastes.

Possibly a few can manage to do this now. But the fact that the arts of the past, as of other unconnected cultures, can provide considerable enjoyment is not enough to justify their indulgence, for impartiality is often well meaning, but rarely effective. One has only to consider the usual attitudes of eclectic art lovers, and the confusions regarding what is contemporary by a well-meaning broadmindedness, to see the tenacity and interference of the past's pull, its promotion of distracting escapisms, romantic nostalgias, and sentimental associations.

The problem is psychological, not reasonable nor amenable to proper education. In order to accept the new fully, one must discard the old completely, a fact which some collectors have discovered for themselves. And the old means the 'Traditional Modern' as well, nay, particularly.

The rejection of so much that is to all appearances 'modern' will seem an outrage to many, but let it be said that the most dangerous enemy is he who passes as a friend. A painter like Bratby, who deals after all with the actual environment, and in spite of the limitations of realism, is none the less more valid in terms of today than a painter like Bazaine, who deals with a crumpled naturalism. It is not realism that is being attacked. It is naturalism in any form, or smuggling, for it plays upon a spectrum of appeal which is no longer relevant to man's actual condition and to the emotional problems facing him, and any kind of appeal to it is bound to distract and block a thoroughly contemporary reacton.

Characteristics of validity

As far as one can see at present, there are about a dozen distinguishable kinds of valid painting today, each requiring a different technique and approach, and no doubt referring to some particular aspect of modern feeling. There are, however, certain features which these all share in common. If one finds any glimmer of traditional appeal in a painting, in spite of the injection of some valid characteristics, then the image is emotionally contaminated. The conditioned reflexes of the past are so strong that they will clamour for priority and reclaim the entire image to the traditional field. Compromise paintings are to be ruthlessly rejected.

Perhaps the most evident trait in the new painting is a disdain of painterliness, of 'good' painting in the traditional meaning of the term. This does not necessarily mean sketchy, hectic, slovenly use of paint, although it can mean that as well. The marks of the journey of the paint are respected as evidence of honesty, the primary appeal of the materials used is extolled, delicacy and nuance avoided.

There is no drawing or sketching as a preparation to painting; no transposition is possible. To avoid being dictated to by intention, to avoid the settling out of a definite structure and statement, many techniques have an inbuilt destructiveness, a continual breaking up of the paint, a prevention of the cooling-out shape, so that the work can be kept 'alive', 'fresh', continually groping.

The line is never used to define shape and form, as in traditional painting and drawing. It now symbolizes energy, and is entirely calligraphic. Although Oriental artists have used the line in this way for centuries, it is exceedingly difficult for Europeans to pull it off successfully[59]. The very importance of drawing in the traditional sense impedes them; so it is that drawing today is more or less entirely dismissed.

To avoid the choice of one particular colour, many artists do several paintings together. This not only enables the imagery to work itself out in its various possibilities—there is always a batch relationship—but it enables a better post-creative selection, and in the new painting, selection can but be post-creative, since there are no pre-set references, no pre-established criteria which one can correct against as one goes along. This way of working also avoids the problem of what colour to choose; a variety of colours can be covered in a batch of paintings done together.

Whereas colour is used melodically in traditional painting, now colour is used as a thing in itself, not to create a musical, orchestrated effect, but as a mark.[60]

The fight to freedom meant at first a smashing up of all evident structure, evident in Pollock. Structure has progressively reappeared, but the only structure which is valid is *synthetic*. It might be argued that nature has tried out every possible structure and shape, that true synthesis is nigh impossible. It is not only the visible form that decides this issue, but the *manner* in which it is built. If one builds up a structure methodically, by traditional technique, one invariably gets a naturalistic, external structure, whereas if one builds up with an avoidance of superimposition, with brashness and a certain imprecision, one gets a quite different form, dynamic instead of static. Of course, any readily recognizable natural shape should be discarded, but it must be pointed out that many people today are figuratively preconditioned by a long cultural process, and tend to see 'things' in most situations, however non-figurative. With much seeing of the new painting, this tendency is corrected, and then indeed the opposite can happen— one ceases to pick out figurative shapes even when they are there!

The term figurative is not appropriate for this kind of independent, synthetic structure in that it stands for natural, external form. Nor is it non-figurative, for it has form. It would be better to use the term 'synthetic figuration' or simply 'synfiguration'.

One must distinguish carefully between genuine energetics and the hotted-up effects of Abstract Impressionism. Pepping up paint in splashes and dripples as in much of 'tachisme' is visibly connected with a naturalistic emotion: nature is tachiste in many of its effects. The only way that paint can be validly used in a spotty, dribbly manner is when it is part of a synthetic structure.

It is the energetic, tense way of working that creates the particular feelings of 'space' and 'time' in the valid image. 'Near', or a fast experience of time, is engendered by active zones, 'far', or a slower passage of time by less dynamic areas, and both are variable in the entire image. Actually, words like 'near' and 'far' lose their external meaning, for the whole image is one activated 'field', in which it is variable events, rather than isolated objects, that create the sensation of being. One can say that space and time are correlated, and both acquire a quite new dynamic reference. It is this that makes a distinct separation between the essential features of the new painting and even the most abstract forms of traditional imagery: the space of 'hard edge', and its time, are definitely separated, externalized, static, not dynamic.

In a traditional image, time is stopped, 'the hushed eternal moment', which is possible only with a view of time which is fixed and regular. A sense of time change, as of motion, can but be illusional; nothing ever really moves in a traditional image. Now motion and the passage of time are directly symbolized by the relics of energy, of the passage and manipulation of the material, and the relics of action are respected because of this.

It is this quite new dynamic space and time of the new paintings that make them radiative rather than enclosed; the traditional painting is always a part of something else, condensed, bounded, a process enhanced by the frame, but now the tensions and energies within the painting tend to radiate out into the entire environment, and the frame becomes an impediment to it. In this sense, the traditional definition of the painting as an isolated object is obsolete. The work of art acquires a quite new dimension and becomes the ideal and only means of activation and emotionalization of the entire physical environment, its supreme humanizing function.

Orthodox psychology proceeds, like the deterministic sciences generally, by analysis and isolation, and so there is a tendency to talk of such things as 'conscious' and 'unconscious' influences in art making. The creative act is one entire whole, and it is only the isolating, interfering habits of analysis and of reason that tend to pick out separate aspects and processes in it. And it is equally wrong to talk of a lack of all determinism or of hazard, for structure and order appear. Rather, determinism is dynamic and order actualized rather than predetermined. The valid imageries today are no more internally, imaginatively, psychologically, predetermined than they are externally conditioned. This is important, for it makes it difficult for the psychologist to handle or even discuss them—they are beyond a dissecting, analytical psychology, and this makes one realize how far removed these paintings are from Surrealism, and from the paintings of the Cobra group, which are full of psychological evidence, and are indeed built up from either vaguely conscious or unconscious external or archetypal prototypes within the mind. The new imageries are synthetic both in an internal and in an external sense.

It might be objected that if they are to have any human meaning, then they must contain recognizable levers to such meaning. This stems from a misconception of the true function of any work of art. It is never a finished thing which is to be merely examined: it is primarily a screen on which the observer can exercise his own creativity. If there are definite levers and guides, then this individual recreativity is limited, and can, to some extent, be analyzed and psychologized. If it is free and open, as are the new paintings, then the recreative experiences are themselves free and work beyond analytical levers.

Only a psychology that had moved from the 'psychology of lumps' to a 'psychology of points', to borrow a term of Karl Menger from modern physics, could deal with such paintings.

7

THE NEW PAINTING

Expressionism: the break with nature

EXPRESSIONISM makes use of paint in a bold, incisive, non-painterly manner, and so produces the entirely autonomous human mark, a gesture of separation and defiance against nature. Colour is unmelodious, a shout more than a song, and the line is a trajectory of movement, not the boundary to a form. Arrange a gradation of pleasing colours on a palette, and daub them on to a white canvas with a painterly use of the brush, working them together here and there, discreetly blended by the greys that form, and you have an 'impressionistic' result. Now take two opposing primaries, say red and green, and holding the brush as if it were a knife or dagger, force the paint boldly on to the canvas and separate the haphazard jabs by black, and you get a distinctly 'expressionistic' effect.

It is this basic difference in technique and in emotional appeal that tends to make the traditionalist miss the meaning and impact of Expressionism entirely, to dismiss it simply as not painting, and, of course, it is anti-painting in the traditional sense, yet the innate tendency of the Expressionist mark to be free from shape and appearance—one can see this in even the figurative Expressionists like Munch—enabled Expressionism to show the way to a total freedom from nature, from appearance, and from external relationships.

Although at the moment of writing there is a temporary reaction against Abstract Expressionism following its enormous successes, it has become none the less the most widely distributed example of the new painting and seems closely related to the mood and feeling of industrial civilization. In spite of repression, it has its practitioners even in Soviet Russia, and is openly practised in Poland and Yugoslavia today.

Abstract Expressionism shows some of the most important

characteristics of the new painting in its clearest light; it is not only synthetic, but its method of elaboration is entirely spontaneous, hit-or-miss, all-or-none. These are so opposite to traditional methods that an analogy is useful, and this is forthcoming in the computer.

Expressionism as a computed function

The fact that we can recognize a given object from a vast number of different angles involves a very rapid computing of visual data; if we had to rely on conscious, rational analysis of such data, we would spend many long minutes before we could recognize anything, and so an intuitive mechanism of exceedingly rapid decisions exists in the human brain which incessantly computes neural information of a very complicated and variable nature. The brain is, in fact, a well-established and highly versatile computer, and it was that long before the emergence of reason and analytical examination. Reason is not happy about giving such a mechanism its due, for it is an innate characteristic of reason to deny all other forms of knowing, yet the inefficiency of reason is well put in the following passage by Lorenz.[61]

> This superiority is due to the fact that intuition, like the highly differentiated types of Gestalt perception, is able to draw into simultaneous consideration a far greater number of premises than any of our conscious conclusions . . . practically unlimited . . . the most important advantage of intuition is that it is 'seeing' in the deepest sense of the word . . . it does not only find what is expected, but the totally unexpected as well.

In the traditional image, decisions are analytical; in the new painting, they are intuitively computed, and the way in which a consistent, orderly, and highly integrated image is built up would be quite outside the much slower analytical mechanisms of reason. The ideas presented by Neumann in his *Theory of Games* are more relevant, as is the recent interest of science in such things as auto-regulative processes in machines and chemical systems, and in cybernetics and ergonomics. The old view of seeing 'conscious' and 'unconscious' influences disappears, and the entire creative act becomes one integrated computation, involving the entire soma, psyche, and substance employed.

One can also understand that speed can be helpful in bringing about this essential involvement with one's material—the entire *raison d'être* of 'action painting'—and in overcoming analytical interference and allowing the intuitive functions to take over. If this way of working can easily pass over into unnecessary showmanship and acrobatics, the pipe-smoking artist is not likely to be able to pull it off, and Expressionist artists are usually themselves dynamic, restless people.

Expressionism and society

As already mentioned, the complete contradiction of painterliness in this kind of painting tends to make the traditionalist reject it summarily as not painting at all. Yet if such a conditioned prejudice can be discarded, it is seen to have a powerful 'existentialist' appeal; it is the typical art of a harassed humanity, the autonomous human reaction against nature whenever nature has turned against man, and it is today the most typical art of an anguishing and precariously surviving culture under the threat of atomic annihilation. It is not easy art; it cannot be readily understood, and cannot be understood at all in the light of reason. If one is not in the mood, if one is hostile and refractory to it, then there can be no appeal at all. It is entirely an art of an instinctive, penetrative nature, of humanity in a penetrative sense.

The slur of morbidity levelled against Expressionism comes in good part from the fact that the usual trivial, hedonist, effort-resisting attitude of people is repelled by any depth-appeal. To be light-hearted is to be 'normal', to see into oneself is to be pathological, even if it is truth that one sees. But it is true that in touch with the harassed, tensed, existential soul of modern man, Expressionism can easily run into the morbid and psychopathic. As psychiatrists have never stopped emphasizing, there are no boundaries between the normal and the pathological in the realms of the mind.

Abstract Expressionism: Vitalism

One always judges vitality by what amounts to a symbolization of it, for the underlying processes of life only concern the scientist. As a result, any object that moves, alters its shape, or appears tensed, alert, 'organic', can be seen as symbolically alive. We think as reasonable people that we know better, yet we are repeatedly confronted with sudden inanimate situations that appear alive, a piece of machinery, a meaningless scratch on the wall, just as to the primitive the river is alive.

A simple blob or line can be seen as vital—provided it is done with vitality. It is a law that a mark can only symbolize the energy that has gone into its making. It is amazing how difficult it is to fool the eye in this respect. Even if a vital line is most carefully copied, even photographically reproduced, it appears somehow less vital, and any mark made with careful deliberation is bound to be 'dead'.

The reason for this is that the dynamic, vital line invariably retains remnants of the dynamic passage of the instrument used, even if it be the finger, in minute flurries and raisings around the edges, in minute granulations to which the eye is particularly sensitive and which become flattened out in the print and which it is quite impossible to copy in the more laborious applications of material.

The elaborate rituals of the Oriental calligraphers were aimed at promoting the right conditions for this vital touch, not by violent and speedy attacks which the European has found necessary, but in far more disciplined yet verveful ways. Generally, as soon as the European artist slows down the line dies out on him, the result of several hundred years of mimetic techniques and attitudes.

It follows that the more complex the image, the more difficult it is to maintain this vitalizing power, hence the importance of destructive aspects in technique which keep the image alive and moving and unfixed. If one can produce a vital image with a few lines, to build up a structure which is both vital and yet structural is a much tougher proposition. If one tries this by traditional techniques, which isolate form and enhance solidity, one invariably ends up with a structure which is dead, for as form condenses free energy is removed, mopped up, and one can state this as a virtual law: the more form becomes defined, the less free energy can be symbolized in the painting. But by the new techniques, which bring in the tensed, dynamic touch, the raw qualities of paint, the refusal to be precise and painterly, one can build up a structure which retains a quivering quality. Here energy is no longer free, but it is intimately associated with a form which is itself dynamic. This association of energy and structure, both dynamic, enables the energy in art to be raised to quite new and intense levels, in the new synthetic figuration, perhaps the highest and most difficult kind of painting today.

When painters first discovered the appeals of the simple splash and dribble a couple of decades ago, there was an orgiastic indulgence in it, but the challenge now is just this—to produce higher levels of energy, energy in more evolved, organized form. Living things provide an analogy; the teeming life under the microscope is the free kind of simple vital energy, the tensed energy in the myonemes of muscle expresses the more organized and powerful kind.

To build up this kind of highly energetic structure a great verve is essential, and must be maintained and even increased as work goes on, and this is why continuous destruction is as important as creation to prevent the crystallization of the image, and it is because of this that the big work is the real test and challenge. It is, in fact, impossible to get full steam up in a small painting; in some way or another, the result is always less expressionistic, more impressionistic.

The difficulty of keeping up this verve is so great that one finds artists reacting to the cooling down in a variety of hysterical, angered ways, but in spite of this, if the drive is not genuine and integrating, there are all the risks of fall-back into some sort of static figuration, either derived from nature or from within the mind, archetypal, anthropomorphic. One finds both these things happening in a painter like de Kooning, in Appel, in DuBuffet, in Jorn, and the very many painters who do not quite make the grade to a synthetic figuration. De Stael reached a near autonomy, but fell back to a weak figuration shortly before his death.[62] It is an ominous indication of the miscarriage of English taste that the bulk of the paintings of this period are apparently in English collections. The French realized early their inherent failure, but not the English critics. On the contrary, the flimsiness of the last paintings met with English taste, and the chronic hoping for some sort of naturalistic revival.

In achieving a highly vital yet synthetic structure a remarkable phenomenon occurs; although entirely synthetic and in no way derived from internal or external nature, the image is felt to have not only an intense vitality but a profound human meaning, and although one cannot give externally descriptive titles to such paintings, one can find in them poignant instances of man's ageless drama, the battles of the spirit and the ascension of the gods, the climaxes of passion and the peals of joy and great moment. One is no longer limited to quite meaningless titles, for here the human drama is outfolding, and man, in abandoning nature and faced at first only with synthesis, has come the circle round to discover a new meaning to life on quite a new plane of actualization.

To most people nothing could symbolize vitality and life better than nature, but if it is borne in mind that all vitality is symbolic, that art trades in this symbolism and has always been able to do better than nature in this respect, one can readily see that the work of art can come to express degrees of vitality with a deep human meaning far more intense than can ever be found in nature or in its imitation in art. So it is that a completely synthetic art can become the highest expression of vitality and meaning. This is most fortunate indeed, for if the artist had been left only with the possibility of using the prototypes of nature in art, he would never have found a painting vital enough to reclaim the synthetic and nature-free environment of the modern world, and mankind would have been condemned to an environment always less emotionally vital and meaningful than nature. As it is, and thanks to this art, the synthetic environment can be made more vital, more meaningful than nature could ever be to modern human beings.

The real dilemma of figuration as opposed to non-figuration is this: although the essential symbolism of art has always been potentially separable from figuration, and although this separated symbolism in a quite abstract art can provide much excitement, a poignant sense of beauty, harmony, and rhythm or what you will of a painting, there does remain the fact that the entire experience of the human race so far in such specifically human experiences as tragedy and drama has been figurative. Can these appeals be put over in a non-figurative way? The answer must be no, at least not adequately. They are emotions which do appear to be genetically connected with form. But before the defenders of figuration cry victory, let us ask one more question. Must the form be naturalistic, or can it be synthetic? Until recently all artists and critics would have answered that in some way structure and form must be replicative, either referring to nature or to mental archetypes or prototypes, in order to have meaning. Today, with the proof of a quite synthetic formal art before us, we know that this is not so. It is indeed a curious and striking fact that formal rearrangements of natural form, nature-scramblings and distillations, as one finds in Abstract Impressionism or in Cubism or Constructivism, end by being dramatically anodyne: they visibly lack dramatic tension, they are bled of tragedy. It would seem therefore that this ability to portray drama and tragedy in form is not at all superficial, although it is associated with visible things in nature, with faces and forms, but on the contrary it comes from the depths which are in themselves 'abstract' formally and symbolically, and so can be most effectively transcribed in painting in purely symbolic or synthetic form. The importance of the new synfigurative painting comes from just this fact: just as this painting is the most suited for rendering an enhanced vitalism necessary for the modern scene, so it is the most suited for rendering an enhanced existentialist dramatic message for modern man.

'Cool' Abstract Expressionism

If the passion falls down, but a tension is maintained, one comes upon a special kind of Expressionist image, not vitalist, but tense, fibrillated, intertwined, charged rather than dynamic, always done with dash and never with fiddling. Soulage is an example of failure to attain this kind of image, for his technique, although brash, is traditional, superimposed, and his space is thoroughly classical and static. It seems to be especially difficult for the European to pull this off, for cooling down seems to mean invariably a static image, deliberate and pedestrian.

Abstract Expressionism: its existential quality

Anguish and travail have always been a part of the anxious European mind, the barely realized failure of reason as a reliable faculty to show man his place in the Universe, the sense of drama, the feeling for the ominous, sinister and malevolent aspects of life and the pathetic situation of modern man; this is a deeply felt although barely describable thing, a situation full of weight and meaning which sponsors a certain quality of greatness and nobility, as well as fear at times amounting to panic, something deeply human and not merely negative like pain and suffering. The Existentialist writers have expressed it as well as one can in words, and it is there also in Abstract Expressionism, in all of it to some extent, but accentuated in a particularly sombre, ominous, mysterious variant.

Abstract Expressionism: the magical and sinister

World Expressionism shows that if it can be life-giving and invigorating, it can also be grim, cruel and sinister, evil. The reasonable mind tends to reject these as unpleasant, even revolting, yet the world is full of evil, a fallen world needing redemption, and magic is as old as man as a redeeming device, the attempt to reconcile the internal, fantastic, and often not very respectable desire of the fallen human soul to a material existence that ignores its desires. The mischievous, the devilish, the Dionysian, the anthroposexual, the flagrantly erotic are most easily expressed in embodied form, but a quite abstract 'magical art' is also possible; it has been practised from the earliest times, by the most primitive of men.

The calligraphic image

Although some philosophers, attempting to serve science, have tried to purge all emotional meaning out of language, all human language has an inseparable symbolic core, and it is this open symbolic quality that enables it to change so endlessly and assume so many forms in dialects and tongues. The symbolic and emotional appeals of writing, for instance, have tended to be neglected in our materialistic culture; they are very important to other peoples, to the Chinese, to the Arab, as they were to the Romans and Greeks, and to medieval people in their magnificent illuminated manuscripts.

Certain Western painters (such as Tobey, Al Copley, Mathieu) have rediscovered this lost faculty, and in abstracting the literal uses from it have elaborated an entirely synthetic language.

Its essence is that it generates, as in the scroll, a sense of time, of continuity, a stream of variable emotional experience that one gets, in fact, from any reading, even of an incomprehensible language. It is fluxal, pulsating, throbbing, paroxysmal. There are several varieties of it, linear or more assembled in complex weavings, and a connexion with the Zen attitude to the transcending power of the simple mark can be felt.[63] It can also pass over to an invalid dither, either 'impressionistic' as in some of Tobey's paintings, or agitative and pathological, the kind of disturbing movement of the line one finds in the drawings of schizophrenics and after taking mescalin.[64]

The semantics of vision

Semantics means significance, and this in art is attained by the emergence of order. As in music, order can be attained by regular and variable time, by repetition, so in a painting the regular repetition of some simple motif can lead to a complex overall pattern-structure. A die or stamp can be used to eliminate the human touch altogether, so eliminating all risks of painterly interference.

The kinetic image

Illusional movement in any form is classical. The new imageries symbolize movement directly in the dynamics of paint, of the materials as used, or by inbuilt moving devices.

Done with sufficiently violent dash different from the 'building up' of Abstract Expressionism, one can leave marks on the canvas like the skids of tyres on a road or the splinters of a ricoché bullet. Actual movement can be brought in as in the 'spatiodynamic' arrangements of Schoeffer, and fire and water can even be used. In the days of the 'magic lantern' ingenious devices were inserted into the projector during intervals and turned by hand, producing a repetitive moving image, and a child's toy, consisting of a lineated image which is made to move against a static lineated counterpart, also produces a sensation of motion. The retinal innervations of closely ruled lines and clashing black-and-white arrangements in Gauguin, Seuphor, Agam, Vasarely, are of this kind, and if they tend towards a simple geometric classicism, they can, when sufficiently complex, acquire a valid dynamic appeal.

The interest of this point has already been mentioned (p. 33), for it means that even if one starts with analytical procedures, one can reach an ambiguous result provided sufficient complexity is embodied into it, and since one always judges the result by its appeal, not by the technique that has gone into it, the result can be valid even if the technique is suspect. The failure of the geometric image and of its present revivals lies in its failure to appreciate the essentials of complexity. Simplicity damns it to an inevitable symbolic classicism. Psychologically, the urge to simplicity unfortunately goes with the geometric preference.

The scroll is an ancient device for bringing movement to the static image, and the motion-engendering power of the cinefilm needs no advertising. The disadvantage is that, like music, performance is necessary, but much room for development of self-contained changing images remains. None of these are illusional, in the sense that implied movement in traditional paintings are illusional (p. 15), for the sense of movement and change is due to direct physiological stimulation, as it is in observing such things as moving machinery, oscillographs, high tension discharges, traffic, in the actual modern environment.

The multiple image

A curiously neglected kind of painting consists of a cellular arrangement of images, which can run in virtually any direction and could thus have great architectural application. It is about the only way of overcoming the rectangular or circular limitations of the painting.

One may well ask why it is that painting is still limited to a rectangular, oval, or circular dimension. The painting is a screen for a projective emotional exercise, and possibly for the same sort of reason that a rectangular shape is the most convenient screen for the cinema, so the rectangular painting is the most appropriate screen for the mental recreation and projection that goes on in art enjoyment.

The unpainterly

It is said that weakness pushed to an extreme becomes a virtue. The clumsy brushwork, the disdain of painterliness, the encouragement of cracks and blisters, the awkward and uncouth shape, the mutilated line, the sloppy scumble, can become positive ingredients in a special kind of image that is special to English painters. If a

Frenchman tries this kind of thing, he does not pull it off. Some of Fautrier's efforts remain highly sophisticated; no doubt a strong tradition of proper training and discipline in art is the hindrance, and the fact that this kind of painting is best done by Englishmen and Americans is the unexpected fruit of a poor art education.

These paintings have been described as expressionistic. But they are not that; awkwardness should not be mistaken for fervour and energy. If anything, they approach more the fiddlings of Abstract Impressionism and they can easily enough pass over to that. It is no relic of bad habits that makes many of these English painters retain naturalistic titles to their paintings, and confess to a continued interest in nature. They are, in truth, against Expressionism, as is the general consensus of English feeling (p. 58).

Matter paintings

Primitive people have a reverence for matter. It has been one of the inconsistencies of European materialism that while it has claimed that matter was the source of all things, it has failed to sense the wonder of such a remarkable agency that can produce life and mind. In recent times there has not only been a change of attitude to matter in science, but technology has produced so many fantastic materials that human beings are becoming alive to the wonder of matter. Man is no longer a mere conjurer, altering, reforming a dead neutral substance; he has become a magician, and artists have not been slow to sense and express this new aesthetic materialism. Most of the valid kinds of painting today use materials thickly, as a visible end in themselves. In one particular type there is an open relish of them.

But there are limits to thickness. As soon as a visible three-dimensional effect is produced, then one passes over to a quite different order, essentially external in its emotional references. The flatness of a painting has indeed a strong emotional meaning in itself, perhaps about the best way of rendering the emotional order of the mind as something quite distinct from the third dimensions of external, physical reality. To move a painting over to a three-dimensional appeal is to negate its most essential quality.

There is also a risk of employing thick materials which have an innate tendency to cakiness and toothpastiness, unless they are used with feeling. Simply to lop them on will not do. And one must be careful in the kind of materials one uses. Although the transforming power of the mind is immense, to use materials with a strong naturalistic appeal, such as hair or wood, is to invite failure to attain a true synthesis. Even stone can be limiting in this respect. Tube paint has itself been used for so long in naturalistic associations that it can fail, hence the imperative of using it in unpainterly ways, and quite new materials such as plastics and lacquers come in handy.

Nor will artificial thickening do. The eye is remarkably sensitive to the honesty of material thickness. If there is the least hint that the thickness does not run through—for instance, if plaster has been used to create the bumps and lumps and then painted over to save paint—then there is an instinctive aesthetic objection. It is to be noticed that this sensitivity of the eye is not the result of culture and fastidiousness; on the contrary, it is the over-sophisticated cultures that tolerate it, in Tutankhamen as in late baroque, but not in primitive art.

The meta image

Every person has caught himself gazing in abandonment at some shining, luminous surface, a glass, a gem, a sunset, water. Time is hushed in a penetrative reverie, one's separation from the objective world is overcome. Necessarily condemned by our critical faculties, it is none the less an extremely vivid experience, and mystics have given descriptions of it. Boehme wrote how he would induce ecstatic trances while gazing at some shining metal object,[65] and a light or a smooth object placed before the eyes is one method of inducing hypnosis.

Paintings with this kind of appeal provide a polar contrast to the energetic paintings, a serene, esoteric calming. They are not paintings to come to lightly in the midst of the bustle of daily living, and require a degree of step back and removal from the busy circuit. They may be thinly painted, and they are worked up slowly, but the slowness never passes over into deliberation and calculation, and technique is not painterly, but rather is minutely destructive, so that a fussing and fluffiness results, giving the paint-film a smokiness and ectoplasmic look.

Forms are incandescent, lumigenic, with clashes of whiteness and sombreness, but black is avoided. This, and the serenity and remote 'sunset feeling' about these paintings, indicate a very distant naturalistic connexion, but like the Zen object, they are metamorphosed and produce an experience which is removed and adequate in itself, usually sudden and paroxysmal.

A very particular mood is required both to create and to appreciate these paintings, an avoidance of rush, a relish in the preparing and handling of one's materials, an empathic attitude.

The flash image

Related to the above, a strong retinal impact is sought by clashing colours, often fairly geometrically arranged. Even if distinct lines are used, and the colours clearly separated, the visual dynamics create a sufficient sense of ambiguity to make this kind of painting valid, provided there is sufficient complexity (see p. 89). Evidently some degree of intention and experiment is required for the clash to work, and the risk is that this sort of painting passes over readily to 'hard edge'.

The hypnotic image

Also related to the above, a quite simple form, usually fairly mistily painted and disturbingly tense and dissymmetric, acquires strong hypnotic appeal. As one gazes, one's emotional plane is suddenly or oscillatingly raised, metamorphosed (hence the term 'meta paintings'), much as the Zen practitioner obtains 'satori' by gazing at certain objects and scenes.

A similar result can be obtained by an image with a visible and clashing dialectic, a dark and a light portion, one section floating in another of quite different texture and colour, a calm and a violently agitated section opposed.

Fields of force

One finds a group of paintings, related to the above, in which tremulous 'fields' of symbolic energy and tension are woven together without overlap.[66] This can easily pass over into a traditional, static geometry, as in Poliakof.

One can find numerous analogies of 'meta' imageries in the new 'landscape' of the urban and industrial environment, in city lights, in sky-glow, in metal and moving machinery, in opalescent plastics. It is also true that sky, cloud, and water are free from organic associations, and so not emotionally naturalistic in the sense that flowers, plants, landscape are naturalistic.

The geometry of imprecision

Euclidean geometry applies to the precise external order of things in drawing and painting. It is by no means the only kind of geometry available for that purpose, as the quite different geometries in Oriental and Egyptian perspective show. But it is the one which appears to go best with the reality-sensations which have preoccupied realist painting since the Renaissance. The Euclidean order fails completely, however, as one moves away from external appearances. The behaviour of electrons is non-Euclidean, and the dream is also outside it. In both these circumstances, the object loses its definition, and acquires a kind of tremulous imprecision, a symbolic ambiguity.

It is a significant observation that as physics and mathematics have been forced to devise non-Euclidean geometries, so art has found the need for non-euclidean expressions, in a persisting geometry which is none the less fluid and imprecise, in the so-called 'soft edge' painting. Here there is no condensing out of definite structure, but zones which are tremulous, to be carefully distinguished from the softening devices in traditional art such as sfumato, the penumbra of shadows or the out-of-focus effects of photography in which normally sharp edges are blurred. In 'soft edge', the entire zone is, as it were, active, and the softening at the edges is due to a greater evidence of it rather than to a blurring.

Any resemblance to a classical geometry is superficial, even if some straight lines and surfaces appear. Colour loses its primary emotional appeal and becomes an agency in the dissolving of form and the precise line, in the convertibility of matter to energy.

The modern environment is rich in 'soft edge' effects, in fast-moving things, in the close-up granularities of printing, in the television screen, and in such commonly used things as X-rays and wireless, which daily demonstrate the inherent 'transparency' of things.

Since the importance and relevance of the paradox is becoming appreciated today, the practitioners of geometric, 'hard edge' painting and their defenders have attempted to interpret their efforts as some sort of ambiguity. But it takes no great acumen to see that these apologetics are in truth intellectual exercises; they have nothing to do with art as a visual phenomenon, for the paintings remain in spite of all the flourish and attempted justification visibly geometric in a deterministic sense, and as such belong to a revival of a now quite ancient image. It is the prerogative of the human mind to project its needs upon external situations, and it is quite remarkable how varied and elastic this interpretation can be on one and the same object. That the need for a sensing of the ambiguous is today ripe and pressing, and in some way no doubt at work in all sensitive persons, cannot possibly redeem a precise geometric image. The fact is that other imageries, specifically new and not revivalist, are far more appropriate, and one can on this count alone predict a short span for the present reincarnated interest in the precise 'hard edge' image.

Machine-made art

The suggestion that an image can occur without the intervention of a human being appears to many as an affront to the dignity of art. Since all art appreciation is a projective function (p. 80), there is however no reason why *any* situation should not be appropriate, whether made by nature, by machine, or by quite incidental agencies like fire or water or chemicals. This creative projection at the basis of all art experience will for ever remain human, as it will always be the human prerogative to accept or reject any art situation.

Only a deterministic view of art and of life need have fear of the challenge of the machine, for the machine can unquestionably do better than man in deterministic fields. But art is not basically deterministic. It is even true that if one had nothing but perfect art, one would reject it for some sort of imperfection. So, granting that projection and choice remain human, to make a division between the man-made and the machine-made object is wrong from the start, and to cherish something simply because it is man-made is romantic bias.

Bringing the machine into the realm of art also brings in a special quality; we are on the threshold of the fantastic, the world of robots, of cybernetics, of machines that reproduce themselves and maintain themselves, and a tremor of apprehension is as excusable as in the earliest men when they discovered the magical powers of ochre on their cave walls. This is unquestionably a new field, a new level of experience.

Robots have assuredly a morbid fascination. They can be an extension of all man's hidden tendencies; there can be robot angels and robot devils, but that has always been the case with anything made by man; the case of atomic energy is pertinent. And there is absolutely no need for the robot to be vaguely anthropomorphic, to look like some bogyman in metal and so to play upon the primitive emotions. The true robot is much more likely to be an assembly of co-ordinated machines, valves, and complex electronic entities, which, by the old laws of functional complexity, will assume an integrated, aesthetic entity of its own.

As for the threat of computers rivalling artists, that could only happens when computers are made which can take good note of the ambiguity and symbolic freedom essential to art. We are a very long way from that at present. It may one day be done, but it will amount to the artificial creation of one of the most elusive and no doubt incalculably complex aspects of mind, an achievement that will be so momentous and fraught with strange prospects for research into the nature of mind and matter as well as art that the artist is likely to be left his creative prerogative.

The chemical image

Effects can be produced on a variety of supports by chemicals, more or less controlled, yet with a considerable degree of spontaneous development: acids on metals, solvents on plastics, plastic resins on various supports. Fire can also be employed to gouge, scour, and destroy by control. The possibilities are nearly inexhaustible, and many are permanent enough for serious work.

The most common chemical image is, of course, the photograph. Even when used realistically, the photograph has certain distinct qualities, which can be varied by many chemical treatments, and a light-sensitive emulsion can be laid on almost any surface, smooth or rough. There is a certain metallic softness about the contrast of light and dark, and enlargements produce singular effects of grain, of out-of-focus aura. It is almost impossible to get a 'hard edge' effect, and except in direct views of nature, the effect is not naturalistic. The emulsion can, of course, also be worked upon directly, by light, by various tools, by chemicals, by montage; in fact, this is a very expressive and all too neglected medium.

Neo-Dada, anti-art

Dada arose in protest rather than in buffoonery. When the time of protest was over Dada declined, as the Traditional Moderns arose and dominated the painting scene. But the rise of just these new masters has spurred various reactions of contempt of authority, with its return of good manners and 'high art', which extends into anti-art. It is particularly the young who feel exasperation at the rising monumentality of 'modern art', and at the fact that the great days of adventure and discovery are over. Some aspects of 'pop' touch upon it.

A genuine neo-Dada art would have an essential anarchical core, an ingredient of rebellion against all that 'high art' stands for. It is not only the recourse to the artistically absurd, the trespass of all convention and good manners, the open courting of the hideous and the malformed, but it can go to the actual destruction of the image, the painting without a painting, from the frame with the empty hole in it to the hanging of an exhibition of blank canvases. Less obviously, it can manifest itself in the painting which is so discreet, so attenuated as to cumulate into a denial of painting, just as a leaching out of colour can amount to a denial of colouristic art.

Real anti-art in one guise or another makes its appearance whenever art tends to overreach itself, to become academically arrogant, sclerotic, and unadventurous, and so threatened with the death of stagnation. In this sense anti-art is a most refreshing and essential function. But it is none the less a negative phenomenon. The moment it becomes positive, organized, obvious, and displayed, for instance in an exhibition, and passed over as some sort of art, then it automatically ceases to have its function; it becomes, in fact, art, just as anarchism can never become organized.

Historical Dada began in anarchic service to a 'modern' art which was fast becoming academic, but to the extent that it was practised by some artists of talent, it soon tended to pass over into art. Today, the anarchism of it tends to be played down, and the art-quantum of it to be lauded, as was evident in a recent B.B.C. Monitor programme featuring Marcel Duchamp, as in a recent book by Richard Hamilton. The mere fact that such notice becomes taken of it means that it is already academic, and much of so-called neo-Dada, displaying the traits of traditional Dada, has come into being without anarchism and rebellion, as a fully fledged variant art-form, somewhat contrived and artificial, often an expedient to find some original twist and clever variant to the visual experience.

Assemblage, Combines, Happenings, Togethers

These are not strictly paintings and verge often into the sculpturesque, but they have been practised from time to time by painters. They must be distinguished from neo-Dada, in that they have no aims external to the making of them, and they are quite seriously practised as art. Although they have affinities with collage, they avoid the traditionalism of it; the results are often crude, jumbled, haphazard.

There is a strictly classical version, in the nicely arranged objects and furniture-like wood structures of Nevilsen. Obviously, such arrangements can but elicit feelings of external relation, whatever surrealist or other affinities they may have. The true assemblage is synthetic. Either the objects or materials used are so dismembered as to be no longer recognized as objects, or uncommon, and therefore barely recognized, objects are jumbled together and so acquire a sufficient autonomy. One cannot fail to detect in some of this a Dada affinity, in the wide searching for the oddest materials so as to bring 'paint' down a peg.

Myth art

Myth is the telling of a story, not in ordinary time, but in a parallel, mythical time, *in illo tempore*, which is nothing but 'internal time'. Since myths belong to one's instinctive being—as soon as they are realized and quite articulate they cease to be myths—we today are not fully aware of our present myths, yet they abound: myths of health and disease, social and political myths, hero myths in entertainment and sport, and those fascinating myths in the cartoons of the daily papers, as well as innumerable myths kept up by the advertisers.

It is possible to have an abstract myth. One has only to make an assembly of bits and pieces, buttons, string, a piece of newspaper, a match, a torn strip of film, and arrange it in a dynamic sequence for it to spin into a 'story'. It is different from the jumble of the 'assembly' in its time-articulation; it must tell a story. The connexions with 'pop' and Surrealism are evident.

A semifigurative or plainly figurative form also appears, vague objects and bodies, a compromise of figuration with valid techniques.

Abstract Surrealism

Surrealism developed as a most important movement among poets and writers, and, perhaps because of its literary origins, it has had less effects on the freely symbolic arts. With practically no influence in music, apart from the visual aspects of ballet, it tended to take a literary form in painting, turning to traditional techniques for minute renderings of space and time, as in di Chirico and Dali, and even in more abstract painters like Ernst and Matta. But it has had a revived influence on quite abstract paintings recently, in the use of lacquers, in shiny, sheeny materials, in the gossamered, beady, tinselly, plush, neonic, iridescent, in a Disney-like half-dream world of strange and faery disembodied happenings. Space is phosphorescent, and time, if it does not come to a classical stop, vibrates in a trance-like state, the time of the drug ecstasy. Technique is neither careful nor is it verveful, but rather masturbatory, flimsy, exciting, often *outré* and with the risks of running to excesses of vulgarity in the taste of the 'boutique' and of 'couturier decoration'.

Simple Art

In an age of exceeding complexity a reactive simplicity in art is inevitable. But this is not the same thing as being naïve; it would be impossible to be that today. Rather, it is the feeling of extreme conciseness, of the purging away of irrelevancies, so that a simple line is felt to contain a world of being. Webern's music is an equivalent of it. Not the simplicity of the child, but the simplicity of the infinitely wise. Simplicity as a means of avoiding the demands of complexity is wrong. Only the simplicity of concentration is valid.

The communal image

The computer-like intuiting that goes on in the making of an Abstract Expressionist image, and no doubt to some extent in every spontaneous image, can be applied to team work. Any number of people, looking at the same thing, could 'compute' synchronously, and provided the participants are emotionally attuned, in interests and attitudes and sensibilities, and provided analytical checks can be cut down to a minimum, a group working together should be able to build up a thoroughly integrated image. As one participant's computation fails, another's takes on, the essential being a spontaneous co-operation; any attempt at apportioning the work is bound to fail. There is a close equivalent in the 'jam session' of jazz. To begin to get involved is the difficult thing. Music can help.

As one would expect, it is the more dynamic types of imagery that are likely to produce the best results.

This is something quite different to the teams the old masters used to depend on to fill in their larger contracts. It suggests that a team could be put to work on very extensive imageries today, in public places, in large spaces in and around public buildings, a truly communal effort. The method also has educational applications, in correcting the tendencies to exaggerate the importance of personality and individualism in creative art. If the individual has his importance, art is also process, in relation to time, to place, to society.

The embracing situation

The traditional image was an isolated instance of the outside world: the new image is a thing in itself which tends to occupy the surrounding spaces by its symbolic radiation and energies. The role of the spectator is accordingly totally different today. In the one he can simply look, in the other he actually participates.

It is only one step more to solicit his active participation. This can be done in many ways, from encouraging him to walk along a scroll-like image along a wall to becoming involved in very elaborate situations and contraptions, in which imageries, sounds, lights, and—why not?—even smells can be made to change and so produce a succession of emotional reactions, infinitely complex.

An essential requirement, however, is that there should be an overall, integrated impression; it is all too easy to produce a disjointed effect. If there are stops, repeats, interruptions, there must be a progressive achievement of ordered sensation and integration, so that, as it were, the spectator is part of an actualizing work of art. It is also necessary that the visual appeals should avoid a traditional 'classical' space.

Abstract realism

Not a contradiction in terms, for if traditional method made possible a move towards the abstract, so present method makes possible a move from the totally abstract to some sort of figuration. Although lacking one important criterion of validity–synthesis and independence of the image from any external reference—such a reversed approach to realism has advantages. Provided it deals with the truly contemporary situation and avoids any backslipping into naturalism and romanticism, and provided the approach is sufficiently free, it can undoubtedly preserve a considerable verve and vitality, a sense of powerful actuality and a dynamic relatedness.

This means that one begins with absolutely independent technique, the student first learning to make a completely autonomous image, and only then moves on to some form of figuration, bringing thus with him some of the badges of technical validity today. It avoids the drabness and dead paint both of 'social realism' and of the 'thick realists', who have done nothing more than to mess up traditional techniques, bringing in mud and technical squalor.

But the figurative appeals must be kept sufficiently discreet not to compete with the free appeals. No doubt one day painters will be able to use external figuration again with much less care and apprehension, but at present the cultural conditioned reflexes of figurative form are still too active. It should also be clearly understood that if some sort of figurative art is likely to return and to provide the more popular imagery, it cannot dominate the scene any more than 'pop' art can do. Popularity and easy access are not the only criteria. Those traditionalists who tend to boost any form of figuration as the means of opposing the new painting should look to their own shadows. The new painting will remain the 'high art' of a more sensitive *élite*, prepared by nature and necessity to put more effort into their aesthetics, for higher rewards.

But not a good word can be said for the present wave of revived direct realism in 'pop' realism in England and America. It is not so much the imagery that is discreditable—any figuration that deals with the actual world is potentially valid—but it is the technique which is no more than a fiddled and incompetent traditionalism, completely devoid of any of the attributes of technical validity.

The English and the Americans feel that they are on to something here, in the battle that is discernibly going on against Paris. The support is, in fact, considerable, but entirely for the wrong reasons. If it is only to be this febrile, contrived realism that is to oppose the Renaissance succession of Paris as the cultural capital of the world, then in all likelihood Paris will retain it. But unfortunately one cannot dismiss it as readily as that, for America today has an enormous influence in the art world, and if that influence is still largely material and so is not, one can only hope, at work in the depths of art, it may well have very tangible if temporary consequences. The real and amazing post-war contribution of America is elsewhere, and certainly lasting; placed against the dogged modern traditionalism of Paris, it is of decisive contemporary importance. But as in England, so in America, retrograde forces are active, and the clamour for some sort of realist return is strong, and is only too visibly pouncing on this ineffective version of it. So, while admitting the legitimacy of an 'abstract realism' that would respect the new acquisitions and visions of the basic art that really matters today, one must guard oneself against the realist usurpers.

8

THE PAINTER AND THE COMMUNITY

The Image in the World

THE aim of all art is communication, and it must surely be the desire of any genuine artist to see his work as widely appreciated as possible, and any other reaction can but be insincere or psychopathic. At present only a very small number of people are even aware of the kind of paintings that have been described in this book. It is not only frustrating to the artist. Formerly, there were other kinds of emotional support, in family and community, and especially in religion; all these have weakened or collapsed. Human beings are emotionally on their own, frail and quite inadequately provided for it. The importance of diffusing a valid art is critical. Wrong art is perhaps worse than no art at all—which is, in fact, the instinctive conclusion of many people who have no art at all in their lives, for it is bound to be emotionally distracting and anti-adaptive.

Fortunately, several forces are working in the right direction. In the very first place, the appeal of a living art is instinctive, whatever the conscious, rationalizing mind has to say about it, and even in spite of persecution and crucifixion, or perhaps because of them, the new works its way through into the instinctive depths. If only people see the new painting, of course. And here again the load is in favour of the new painting, for, if even for the wrong reasons, it is getting around, indeed even in spite of ferocious opposition and official condemnation. There are the positive sides of education, of mass communication—the new electronic music has found its way into advertising, and the new painting is coming in everywhere: in launderettes, in coffee-bars, in waiting-rooms. This is quite a remarkable fact; only a few years ago it would not have been thought possible. What has actually happened is that the instinctive defences are already crumbling, and although people claim not to have any sympathy or understanding for the new imageries, they are handling them, in spite of themselves. It is only a very short step to instinctive acceptance, and then reason can say what it likes.

One can also see another favourable process at work; only a few years ago, it was widely believed, and by some without argument, that what is right for the majority is simply right, and that anything else must be less right or quite wrong. This veneration of mass standards had come to dominate design, management decisions, and many other aspects of life, even in intellectual quarters. There is a visible reaction against this. Dignity, it is being sensed, is best served not by levelling, and the symbols of democratic upgrading are being instinctively taken up by an increasing number of people in all walks of life. And art is perhaps the most visible symbol of anti-entropy, of social up reaching.

Even twenty years ago there could be some optimism in a progressive 'enlightenment of the masses'. Today, pessimism is more frequent, even in Left circles. 'Most mass entertainments' writes R. Hoggart in *The Uses of Literacy*, 'are in the end what D. H. Lawrence described as "anti-life". They are full of a corrupt brightness, of improper appeals, and moral evasions. . . .' Or to quote Hannah Arendt in *The Human Condition*: 'The hope that inspired Marx and the best men of the various workers' movements—that free time eventually will emancipate men from necessity and make the *animal laborans* productive—rests on the illusion of a mechanistic philosophy which assumes that labour power, like any other energy, can never be lost, so that if it is not spent and exhausted in the drudgery of life it will automatically nourish other, "higher", activities. . . . A hundred years after Marx we know the fallacy of this reasoning.' The only alternative to this stagnation in mass values and the only way to continued social evolution is an appeal to forces operating outside, or over and above, the bulk of the population, and it follows as an unavoidable corollary that at some stage or other, imposition or insinuation must be involved. Upgrading effort, and the concept of anti-entropy, are as valid in society as in science.

To many this conclusion would seem to carry the danger of the anti-democratic heresy, of intellectual totalitarianism. But this danger is surely balanced by the fact that the rising *élite* of today—and we must resign ourselves that there must always be one—is classless and socially responsible. There is a greater danger of social corruption in maintaining the false magic which has been associated with mass concepts, with the unimpeachable virtues of the 'common man'. Unfortunately, what is common and popular is almost invariably also anodyne and frequently vulgar, trivial, and, ultimately, antisocial, in that it indulges in the easiest and most static and unenterprising appeals and condemns effort, as is only too plain to see in popular entertainment.

The facts of the case are such that 'great art' is never likely to be a widely popular art. The best that one can expect is that the bulk of people will accept this, and will not be encouraged by misguided intellectuals to oppose the *élite*, to which, of course, they should themselves belong. In primitive communities elaborate initiation ceremonies are required to put people into the right frame of mind before they are even allowed to come into contact with the esoteric objects of art and ritual, and in our recent past a hedonistic view of art has so prevailed that people have been encouraged to believe that all they have to do is to look, that no effort is required, and the truth that all art appreciation is basically recreative is very little realized.

Desperate attempts have been made by artists to impose themselves on the public, usually with little or no effect. What would happen if artists one secret night were to bespatter all those bare, meaningless city surfaces with imageries? No doubt imprisonment. People simply do not want to be bothered by art, or only want it in undisturbing driblets, broken down into soft porridge by critics who prepare the hash as they like it. An elaborate machinery exists for protecting the public against the artist, against the artist who is likely to disturb, to summon an obligation of attention and effort. What, in fact, is the place of the advanced artist in society today?

The influences of nationality

In the past one hundred years some sixteen million people have been killed in European wars, not to count the many times that number who have died as the direct result of war, in degradation, despair, and suffering. In the face of this satanism, it is difficult to pick out the better qualities of nationalism, the summoning of heroism, the self-sacrifice, the patient endurance.

Yet is it evident that this hypertrophied nationalism plays upon characteristics which are deeply human, upon a pool of emotionalism intended by nature no doubt to serve man, against adversity, in making sacrifice and the endurance of hardship possible, a kind of natural ability to pervert love for the ends of critical survival, a process which can easily become pathological, as it does become with the rise of industrialism.

The land of hope and glory goes with the black industrial skies of the Dark Country, and the festerings of the Continent can be traced to the Ruhr and the Donets Basin. In times of trial and tribulation human beings naturally close together; nationalism and crisis are brothers, and if all culture is bound to bring tensions and maladjustments, rivalries and greeds, none has come any-where near in extent and crime to the rising phases of European industrialism.

There are signs that this demonic phase is coming to an end, but it is necessary for us to see the full iniquity of it, for it still shadows us and conditions our feelings and reactions, and still too many people are apt to see only the fair and more noble sides of nationalism.

The hope comes with a correction that arises within in-dustrialism itself. If the earlier phase was entirely ruthless and accaparitious, and was accompanied by ferocious competition both within society and internationally, as industrialism gets under way and passes to the stage of mass production, turning out ever more goods and goodnesses, so it is forced to co-operation, national and increasingly international. Take-overs and increasingly complex industries with innumerable associate companies are not only national; they have now passed on to an international ramification of business, industry, and technology, and a depend-ability on a world-wide array of raw materials. Many Frenchmen and many Germans may still hate each other, but industrialism is forcing them together by its inbuilt impetus.

One can therefore conclude that if nationalism still smoulders in many forms, the trend, inevitable and certain apart from some holocaust, is towards a developing of international feeling. Practical necessities of a self-perpetuating industrialism are certain to achieve what the greatest moralists and ethical persons have lamentably failed to achieve, a universal brotherhood of man.

In the field of art, the trends are all the more obviously inter-national and internationalizing. But one cannot but notice that as this trend pulls one way, there are many people working in just the opposite direction, encouraging and promoting nationalism in art in one form or another. Since strong national feelings still exist, and periodically erupt, such a playing is bound to seem right and popular to many, and an artist who placates such feeling, irrespective of his contribution as art, is bound to receive a measure of acclaim.

One is faced with the dilemma that if mankind is prompted on one side to become humanized and enjoined in communities of ever-increasing size until a planetary community is attained, there are also the inbuilt instigators of division and discord, social, psychological, linguistic, economic. What can be more dividing than language? One has also to do with the exasperating eruption of isolating agencies as a people strive to assert their liberation and dignity, so evident in the outbursts of nationalism in Europe in the past 150 years, and now distressingly evident in the break with colonialism the world over. One of the most civilized of countries, Norway, elects to revive and make compulsory a dialect not native to the majority of the population.

The truth of the situation is that in clamouring for emancipation communities do go through a phase of acerbated aggressiveness and inter-hostility, but that rising socio-economic forces are ironing out these dangers and forcibly fusing the human species into a planetary awareness. This is surely more than a hope: as opposed to the demented discords of politics, one finds a growing scientific and industrial fraternization and interdependence, and such manifestations as 'ban-the-bomb' are symptomatic of a growing paranational consciousness.

The trends are so clearly internationalizing that one can say summarily that any chauvinism in art today is retrograde and bound to run counter to the main trends of art in our times. But having said this, certain national features can enrich and diversify the true international manifestations of the age. It is when nationalism becomes a separating force, a wedge against the main stream, an agency in making falsely different and distinct, that it is to be condemned.

As one would expect from the conditioning of art by environment, the first country to start the industrial revolution, England, was also the first to show the response of change in art. The signs of the Impressionist revolution appear half a century in England before they are taken up in France. Since the move towards abstraction was a continuation of the traditional, the country best schooled in traditional art, France, was the best equipped for it. Puritanical restraints and lack of a well-developed attitude and respect towards painting were the English handicaps.

But the very conditions that enabled the French to take on the development of Impressionism have prevented them from coming to the really new painting, which is a denial of traditionalism on every count. The American painters of the post-war period have been vociferously condemned, and most of them are not as yet represented in leading French collections. To the Frenchman, this kind of painting is not painting at all; it is anti-painting. Whether or not France can correct this handicap remains to be seen. Conditions at the moment of writing are not encouraging. French pride, wounded by a humiliating defeat in war and by a succession of colonial calamities, seems to be engaged on a revived cultural crusade, but along neotraditional lines, which can but be against the new, and with full official backing this could be calamitous to a country which has up to now been the art centre of the world.

Because of their chronic incapacities in painting, the English have looked to the French for leadership and support. But these very infirmities have made them emasculate the French contribution. Although a few English painters might pass as mediocre French professionals, the French themselves are the first to exclaim that English painting lacks the verve and strength, the technical assurances which are characteristic of the French. Qualities hailed in England as virtues in paint are condemned by any French painter and critic, and it is just those qualities that are put over officially in England as the virtues of good taste, of discretion, of a gentle insular civilization and romanticism. In truth, these are nothing but a weakness of vision, an inability to use colour and explicit form, and an emotional emasculation, so that a painting that 'one can live with' comes to mean a painting that makes no emotional demands upon one.

A strong anti-contemporary strain is also due to an insular romanticism, to the graces and gentilities that Englishmen have been able to maintain thanks to their relative isolation from the angers and realities of social and political upheavals on the Continent. Whatever the reasons, a romantic naturalism survives in England today as nowhere else, practised by almost all artists and getting the support of almost all critics and dealers. The St Ives influence has become the most active agent in preventing the English from a contemporary alignment in painting. One cannot help wondering what the effects on painting will be if England joins the Common Market. Can England still manage to play a role in the humanization of the industrial age which it has done so much to bring about?

There has in the past few years been a turn away from French influence among English painters, as the Americans have provided an alternative support. This has received considerable intellectual promotion, for no matter how critical the English happen to be about Americanism, they are secretly proud of it. But as with the French influence, here again there has been an emasculation and an almost total omission of the effusive, raw dynamic power of the Americans. If there has been talk of civilizing the American contribution, what has, in fact, happened is a misapplication of its most important quality, vigour and enthusiasm.

As the English began Impressionism, but failed to develop it further, so the Americans have started the revolution of the new painting—although the initiation and impetus is less exclusively theirs than has been made out—there are growing signs that they are not properly equipped for keeping it going. After the first two big post-war generations, there is little happening among the young. If anything, there are the same dangerous symptoms common enough in England, 'hard edge' puritanisms, and sloppy returns to evasive figurations of one kind and another. Realism, perhaps less rejected even by painters in America than the upsurge of the great post-war abstract painters would indicate, may even make a major comeback, and so knock America right out of the stage of significance. An even more distressing symptom is a growing chauvinism, the arrogant assumption that only American painting now counts. The roots are too young to hold such a big tree.

But perhaps we fail to appreciate the genesis of the American outburst in valid painting; perhaps it comes from deep roots, and after a temporary eclipse will again surge forward. Why, in fact, did it occur in America? Wars always shock into realization tendencies which may have been dormant for long, and the last war has suddenly brought Americans from relative isolation, far worse than any known in insular England, into an acute crisis of planetary responsibility. One can but hope that the responsibility will extend to the great art they have undoubtedly initiated. Right or wrong, with the enormous wealth and power behind its promotions, the American influence is likely to be enormously important.

The influences of religion

Although in decline, the established religions have still an enormous influence on art, an influence which is on the whole unfortunately negative. Catholicism, in having adapted itself to the Renaissance ideology, in relying on Thomism and ignoring the opposite interpretations of St Augustine which might well have been more compatible with the present sensibility, has become the defender of the Renaissance succession into the present day. It is suspicious of all abstract art, as a move from the visible rational order of creation which has become the theological reference, and if recently it has come to accept with considerable reservations the Traditional Modern, it is emphatically unsympathetic to the new painting, and its arguments against it would be very similar to those of the materialists and Marxists: that it is a denial of reality, of humanity, of order.

If Catholicism is at least aware of the challenge of a changed art, and prepared to take a stand about it, Protestantism, with its long traditions of compromise, has no particular attitude to it at all. As in the new Coventry Cathedral, pragmatism and functional clarity make for a certain discernible superficiality. The sensible attitudes of Protestantism make it, in fact, quite intolerant of any ambiguity, although Christian Existentialism appears an exception to this. The pragmatic strains of historical Jewish culture, although more inherently mystical and ambiguous than the Catholic, do not take easily the visible break of the new art with the antecedent rational order. Perhaps more than any other people, and quite understandably, the Jews are fearful of any challenge to reason, for they have suffered most from human irrationalism. If Jewish artists take readily enough to abstract art—like the Mohammedans they have a certain cultural conditioning to it— they naturally appear to favour some sort of figuration and so condemn an all-out, nature-independent abstract image.

The influences of society

In the past patronage has always been in the hands of a privileged *élite*. The bulk of the people had either no choice about what was put to them in the form of religious and national symbols, or else resorted to their own very simple efforts in a world-wide peasant art. Even in quite primitive societies, religious and totemic art is usually in the hands of an exclusive minority.

With the rise of industrialism this process continues in modified ways. The peasant contribution dies out, and most people go without art at all. Led at first by the privileged classes, the rising industrial revolution coincides with the big private collections of the seventeenth century. The progressive dispossession of this class and the rise of the middle classes to power has seen the appearance of the public collections, and these have naturally tended to simulate the levels of taste of the private collectors, the visible symbolization of luxury and the good life. By the mid-nineteenth century this had become the accepted art and taste of the masses. This does not necessarily mean that most of them liked it, or even looked at it, but it had become *their* art, and taste, no longer instinctive in a rising welter of artificialities, soon became a cultural conditioned reflex, further consolidated by education and social attitudes. Without realizing the machinery of this subtle imposition, the people came to accept the ideals of the classicists and of the traditionalists, a conspiracy that has yet to be exposed in full.

In a fast-changing age taste became stabilized in the 'established values', and an art which expressed this was the last thing people wanted changed. But if the many managed this emotional barricading against change, the more sensitive artist failed, and so broke away from a society and from an age that had become largely hostile to what he felt essential to art. Bohemianism was born, at first rebellious in its neglect of social graces and in its debaucheries, and only later made romantic and fashionable.

One might have expected that the new classes of industrialism would have cherished new things, but on the contrary, as the new classes, managerial, skilled, and working, established themselves and their rights in a society that depended entirely on them, as their benefits increased, they fast developed the same kind of defence of the established order one finds in all privileged classes throughout human history. But now this class had become the majority, a majority conservative in feeling and quite anti-revolutionary in every field, most of all in matters of taste.

It is one of the great delusions to believe that revolutions bring in all things new; there is an ignored conservative aspect of every revolutionary movement; evident in post-revolutionary France, and today in Russia, and everywhere in the wake of developed industrialism. Perhaps the full possession of the new can only come when things settle down, when fear passes, when normality returns, when, in fact, new things can become orthodox, traditionalized in their turn. Such is the human constitution.

The conclusion one can draw from these mostly negative considerations is that the new painting cannot expect a wide and easy applause; on the contrary, in all the arts that really matter, opposition, and even persecution, are certain. Perhaps there is a masochistic strain in all progress, in the promotion of all new things, which makes it necessary, and which provides a whip and stimulus in the oppression; but one thing is certain, if a person desires acclaim and popularity, if he desires only to be loved because of his art, as Freud claimed, then he had better keep to the traditional. The new art carries a flame.

But if the new art cannot count on prevailing and popular support, it can count on an *élite*, which exists now and is ever on the increase, a new 'open aristocracy' of more sensitive people from all over the world, of all races and backgrounds.

Art and politics

Some of the leading artists in the modern movement in painting from Delacroix onwards have been actively involved in politics, invariably of the Left. The new art has felt itself serving a new age, and has been an ally of all change from the old order. In the past the figurative painter has been a useful tool to the politican. Picasso's *Guernica* has done a great deal for the cause of the political Left, and one can see that the politician has no use for a non-figurative art, useless to him for propaganda. The Pope had a similar interest in Michelangelo.

But political disclaim has failed to halt the rise of abstract painting by painters with Left sympathies. In a country like

France, where the free traditions of painting are so strong as to weigh against any doctrinal ruling, Communist painters have found some way of continuing an art of inner necessity which runs counter to official ruling. Elsewhere, where art has been more traditionally bound, doctrinaire rulings have had more effect in restricting artists, as in Soviet Russia. But even there, the heralds of a greater liberalism in the arts are evident today. It would seem that in the clash of art and politics art is winning.

The fact that artists can be apparently Left in spirit and outlook and yet produce an art which is condemned by the political Left comes from the fact that 'Left' and 'Right' in the mind and in actual practical politics are not at all the same thing. Professor Flugel[67] made a list of the opposite characteristics of the psychological 'Left' and 'Right'—the appreciation of change, the opposition to it, the discarding of conventions and traditions and the respect for them. The one is compatible with progress, the other with stability and a dislike of change; the one with social justice, the other with a respect for privilege. Evidently, one would expect that a psychological 'Left' and a political Left would be one and the same thing. That they can be, but usually only in the fervours of change, in the idealistic peaks of revolutions. As soon as conditions begin to settle down, then people of apparent Left political affiliations develop 'Right' psychological traits, so that there is a growing disparity between the psychological and the political. In fact, one finds nominally Left political parties and entire societies which display many psychologically 'Right' characters, just as one finds psychologically 'Left' notions in political parties of the Right when change becomes essential or expedient.

There can be no doubt of it that the new art should be encouraged by and in entire accord with the psychological Left; it was so in Russia for a short period after the revolution, and it only becomes condemned when the revolutionary society begins to settle down and psychologically 'Right' trends to appear—authority, patriotism, revival of tradition. The fact that this condemnation of the new art has been defended on intellectual grounds should deceive no one. The argument that only an art readily understood by everyone, or an art that bears an obvious social message is valid runs against the entire history of world art and all that one has come to know about its psychology. The real cause for the defence is psychologically 'Right', a fear that the new art is a threat to the stabilization of the revolutionary ideas which have become, in fact, orthodox.

The creative artist, exploring the new and adventuring in the offerings of change, can but be 'Left' psychologically, and, of course, if the political Left fitted with the psychological Left, he would as naturally be politically Left; the break between painting and politics occurs when the politics of the Left is, in fact, betrayed and corrupted. It is politics that change, not the artist, and perhaps the greatest predicament of the artist today is that if he feels his emotional affinities for what the Left could and should stand for, he finds it impossible to subscribe to many of the activities of the political Left, its anti-individualism and especially its condemnation of the one kind of art which tallies with the revolution of our times. To talk of a 'dictatorship of the Left' is a thorough confusion of terms: dictatorship is a 'Right' psychological trait, the expression of the belief that the enforcement of law, of belief, is justified, and to associate it with the Left is a complete debasement of that term. The genuine Left can but be liberal, never coercive.

One of the main causes of this failure of the Left is the corruption of Left ideology, by politicians of the so-called Left. The subsequent corruptions of Marxism are notable and now historical. As a philosophy, Marxism has made many contributions to modern thinking and attitude, its emphasis on the importance of the environment, on the prime cultural importance of science and industrialism, on the social mechanisms of change, on class conflicts. But as a philosophy, it was also founded in an age of rigid determinism and in an age of arrogant scientific materialism. And many of its philosophical deductions have also been proved wrong. Marx paid as little attention to aesthetics as did Freud, and his understanding of the inner mechanism of industrialism was superficial. It is a curious thing that while Marx realized the decisive importance of environment on the human condition, he should have missed so singularly the role of art in a period of change. Since active politicians and political thinkers are seldom refined philosophers, much of Marxism has been crudely adapted to serve ends which are not so much Marxist as political in a very retrograde sense of the word, and political Marxism has shown itself singularly incapable of adjustment and revision. Here one is head on with a character which is typically 'Right', the stubborn, bigoted defence against change. In many respects, another institution with mostly 'Right' psychological characters, the Catholic Church, has shown itself more adaptable, no doubt through a much longer historical experience of psychology, of authority and rule.

The tragedy of the rise of the various forms of political Marxism is that they have devoured and demolished the idealistic liberal socialism that had preceded them. The tragedy can no doubt be blamed on the upheaval of the times themselves, for a humanistic socialism that would respect certain preserves of the individual and of his place in society failed to cope with the angers and hatreds of the rising social injustices and the initial chaos of the industrial revolution, particularly on the Continent, where a fearful and entrenched privileged class fought change with a heartless cunning which has been largely avoided in countries such as England, America, and Scandinavia, thanks to a long liberal tradition.

All aspects of life and all institutions were affected by this ruthless inner struggle, drawing out increasing hatred and violence in its oppositions. As an example, if Freemasonry continued in humanistic forms in the Anglo-Saxon countries, on the Continent quite different and antihumanistic forms appeared, frequently involved in the large-scale organization of violent political action.

For the artist, the collapse of the humanistic Left and the rise of ruthless travesties of Marxism is a tragedy. The situation is somewhat different here between the painter and the writer. The painter has sensed the betrayal, but many writers do not appear to have done so, and still serve the political Left in various ways. What the writer, as an intellectual, is interested in is not the underlying emotional, psychological aspects of the 'Left', but its intellectual satisfactions and aims, which can persist even when the emotional fire is dead. The kind of arguments one still finds in such circles, of the virtue of political action today, betray a schism between feeling and intellect which is meaningless to the more emotionally conditioned artist.

But one finds many truly creative writers and poets aware of the betrayal of the political Left, and showing as a result all the signs of a lack of political interest. This is indeed symptomatic of out times. Although changes are visible in the Marxist hegemony, anyone who knows something of the background cannot help doubting whether there can be sufficient change and adaptation for the doors to be opened to a real freedom in the arts. Fortunately, there are signs that even in the Marxist countries today there is a declining reliance on the ultimate virtue of political action and servitude. It is, as it were, a growing world-wide realization in industrial society, not only of the betrayal of politics, but of an increasing awareness of the uselessness of it. It is a statistical fact that people are losing interest in politics, a fact which those of the former generations of violent political action and commitment find exasperating and verging on blasphemy. People are naturally concerned with getting ever more of the good things of life, television sets as well as medical care, cars as well as old age pensions, and the point is that these are being realized today not by political intervention, not by removing it from one privileged and grabbing class to share it out more fairly, but by the growing momentum and development of industrialism itself. If any single agency is responsible for the provision, it is the technologists, the scientists, the organizers and managers and skilled workers in industry.

The increasing failure of politics as an effective machinery in both national and international spheres (see p. 67) is having some remarkable consequences; people are having to be bribed to make some show of interest: they either gamble over an election—some fifteen million pounds are estimated to have been wagered on the last election in Great Britain—or they are bribed with bands, parades and low-line girls, tricks which the Americans, far farther advanced along the evolutionary line of industrialism, at least in some respects, have now had to resort to for some considerable time. More and more, people are allowing the politicians to go on playing their antique games as a social diversion and to some considerable amusement: as long as they get the goods of life, people do not much care, and the likelihood is that politics is likely to become either some sort of a public and international charade, or completely obsolete as the new technocracy takes over. The clash between the technocrat and the politician is already inflamed and desperate, and the recurring malaise in Europe now is due to nothing more than this.

One of the most erroneous myths of the last century's political theorists was the importance of the 'masses' and their drive to power; almost all people are much happier led than leading, and when all their wants and more are being satisfied a rush of the libido into channels of power-seeking is most unlikely. The end of revolutions, as of politics, is probably at hand, for like the warrior kings of old, who were the entire providers and protectors and therefore loved by the people, the new technocrats are becoming the entire providers of the new cornucopia and are likely to be so loved. Here, then, lies optimism: in the prospect of an end to national and international politics.

The inbuilt increasing need for co-operation in industrialism has already been mentioned, evident in the international combines, now courting even the Communist bloc, in an ever-increasing pooling of resources and skills. The one-third rich nations are finding themselves obliged to help the two-thirds poor, and instead of thanks are having to take boos and whistles. It is indeed most fortunate that the collapse of colonialism coincides with this obligatory international co-operation and assistance, for in spite of its many evils, colonialism did provide a framework of order. Its collapse is, in fact, far less ideological than necessitarian, just as a rising industrialism made slavery superfluous. In spite of the crippling and unfortunately temporarily increasing miseries and poverties of the present two-thirds poor—food alone cannot keep up with population increase—there is hope, when one thinks of the fantastic and increasing resources of the great industrial centres of the world today. And industrialism has that quality about it that it cannot cease, like some fanatic messianic religion, until the whole world has been thoroughly industrialized. The un-industrialized of today can rest in the confidence that they, too, will be industrialized and so share the planetary benefits of this fantastic new culture, whether they like it or not, but being human, they are sure to like it, and are, in fact, everywhere clamouring for it.

The importance of political involvement is therefore weakening, and the realization of the betrayal of the political Left loses some of its disastrous importance. One cannot shut one's eyes to the persisting poverties and miseries of the majority of human beings; even in the midst of the most advanced industrial countries, much remains to be remedied. It will take a long time yet to convert the world from its fallen state to the heaven on earth which is now promised in man's universal effort. But it is not only a comfort to know that the momentum is increasing in the right direction, but that this achievement is now passing out of the hands of the amateur and provocateur, of the politician who in the past and up to the present has had no other qualifications than a certain amount of ruse and oratorial ability—and now, a television fitness—into the hands of people more especially qualified and capable.

No doubt there is much to be done, and one cannot but admire any and every social and international effort of help, but simple protest in itself is probably useless, and the artist, a kind of social specialist in himself, has things to do for society for which he is especially qualified and which others cannot do. Besides, he is a noticeably unpractical person.

The artist's proper field of social action is art itself. It is simply not true that art has lost all social force and power of action since it has abandoned figuration; it can no longer serve the petty ends of propaganda, but its humanizing and social appeals are extensive.

Art is the one truly internationalizing form of feeling and attitude today. It is the perfect counterpart to the intellectual and pragmatic internationalism of science.

Art is the visible display of the most human and humanizing trait, which requires and insists on freedom for its proper exercise. In following his art the artist necessarily fights for human freedom and gives visible expression to it.

Art is the emphasis of feeling, of life, of desire, of the value of human experience as something utterly unique. It is the opposite of all death, of corruption, of bestiality.

Art is at heart and spirit anarchical in that it is against establishment and authority, against the given and the proved, and insists on a continuation of the open adventure of living.

Art is humanization, made visible, redeeming, purifying.

Art is protest, protest against all that is inhuman and unfeeling, all that is debasing and lowering to human dignity.

Art is the opening of the eyes to the wonder and miracle of the world and of the human presence in it in a continued creative capacity.

And art is many other things.

Art in a sick society

Although usually people are apt to ignore the chronic pathology of existence, the fact is that innumerable forms of ill health, ranging from the barely perceptible to the crippling, are the common lot. Optimism and the blind eye are perhaps fortunate human traits, for the real situation is desperate. There can be no doubt that in spite of medical progress in the treatment of many diseases, others, and those of a more insidious and intractable nature, have increased and have perhaps rightly been called the diseases peculiar to civilization, the diseases of physiological degeneration and of mental distress.

Society can be no healthier than its average members, and in such a state of things society itself and all the human activities within it are bound to show symptoms of physical and mental pathology. They are all too evident. A good deal of this pathology must come from the disturbances of life, physical, mental and emotional, that attend industrial and urban living, profound changes in food, in habitat, in air and water, changes in habits and activity. But whatever the causes, it is most likely that art, like any other human phenomenon, would show signs of the general stress. A glance at world art shows many signs of disease, in the macabre, the horrific, and the frankly disturbing and tormented. And in our own art, there are examples of it.

Disease is most likely to stimulate the more primitive and physiologically connected emotions, and it is also understandable that these should find the figurative the most convenient expression. It is difficult to imagine a disembodied devil, and human-like or animal-like fiends, goblins, or gnomes are world-wide apparitions. When modern art was still figurative many instances of pathology were to be found, not only visibly horrific, morbid paintings, but paintings unwhole and fractured with their disturbing emotions. But the advent of an abstract art has removed one of the main ways in which art can give evidence of the diseased and harassed spirit, and no doubt one of the reasons for its emergence is just this need to go beyond the embodied disturbances of a satanic and demented age.

In going abstract and dispensing with figuration, the full and enormous powers of art for integration and wholeness, for harmony and a co-ordinated symbolism, can come into play. One can see this at work in quite seriously mentally diseased persons: their powers to find an instinctive order in an abstract jumble of bits and pieces put before them remains, often into advanced disease. If however, they are led to give figurative expression in drawing and painting, then the results are much more likely to show the signs of stress, and the fact that many psychotics show a natural tendency to go towards abstraction is due to the fact that they instinctively strive to avoid the figurative distress and grope for the enwholing forces at greater play in the abstract. And it is for such reasons that art today has become an established part of psychotherapy.

An accentuated symbolic activity accompanies many mental diseases, the inevitable accompaniment of an emotional life stimulated by pathology. It is this that makes mentally disturbed persons aware of things which ordinary people pass unnoticed. These processes themselves, like the increased symbolic functions, are not necessarily diseased in themselves: they are merely made more apparent in disease, and through disease. Because of the natural tendency for any such accentuation to take a more purely symbolic, 'abstract' turn, this has been pounced upon by the attackers of abstract art as proof that abstract art is itself a malady. This it can, of course, be, but in fact it seldom is, for the whole-striving tendencies of the mind find their greatest support in such an abstract exercise, and art makes what is a potentially distraught and unbalanced whole.

What actually happens is that the mentally sick person cannot give proper and whole expression to the underlying and essentially normal processes of symbolic accentuation going on in him; his expression itself is pathological, fissured, unwhole, a lack of organicity so evident in the paintings of schizophrenics. Neurosis, on the other hand, not only leads to an increase in the symbolic awareness, but is accompanied by an increased power to reveal it in whole, integrated and antipathological ways.

The integrating power of art need not stop there. The psycho-somatic problem today is widely recognized, and if the body works upon the mind, so the mind works upon the body, in both the negative sense of disease and in the positive sense of recuperation and healing. One of the emotional, psychosomatic effects of nature upon human beings since the dawn of human creation has been the invigoration and vitality that nature symbolizes, in green growing things, in the turgors of branch and bud and the promises of health and joy in fruits, in the vitality of animals and in a general throbbing and pulsating of all living things. In health, man is part of this, and the tension of vitality is shared by him. Not properly conscious, this inner state of relationship, of the wholeness of well-being and abounding vitality is none the less keenly appreciated and sought after by all primitive peoples, and whenever it is threatened there are an endless variety of rituals and sacrifices, medicinal and magical, to attempt to restore it.

Within the mind and body there are evident mechanisms of stimulation and restoration: when vitality fails there is a reactive restlessness and agitation, mental and physiological, especially sexual. This has obviously been the case with industrial, urban human beings, part of the mechanism of inner motivation to industrialism we have already mentioned. But it is also a fact that this reaction is in good part if not entirely misdirected as far as the restoration of physical and mental balance are concerned. The reason is clear. Under the highly artificial conditions of modern life, the whole-making, integrating influences from nature are entirely lacking, and so the reaction is itself unwhole.

Health is integrated physiological and psychological function, the body and mind working as one efficiently integrated unit, a harmony of united function achieved by long evolution and selective perfectioning. Any agency or change which alters the established patterns of genetic normality—food is the most complex and permeating possibility of interference, apart from parasites and bacteria—there is reaction, disease, elimination or recovery. If the change is within the genetic experience of the animal's past, then the reaction is likely to be efficient. If the alteration is new, the animal has no genetic equipment to deal with it and chaos is more likely than not, and there may even be no warning mechanisms of distress at all. This is just what happens in the case of the so-called civilization diseases; a disease like cancer can make much rodent headway before any symptoms are noticed, and the response of the body is negligible. Cancer is, in fact, a relatively 'new' disease in its wide prevalence.

It is feasible that in cases of inefficient and chaotic reaction to abnormalizing agencies, vitalizing and whole-making influences such as art can help through the psychosomatic connexion. It is a fact that can be readily experienced by anyone that the contemplation of vital art can induce a kind of enlivening, quickening experience akin to the feelings of abounding health. Art, as the ancient Greeks believed, has therapeutic possibilities. It is not naïvely suggested that simply by looking at vitalistic paintings diseases of the mind and the body will be healed, but it is claimed that an environment in which powerful symbolic foci of vitality and wholeness abound will aid the body's own inadequate and unwhole reactions. In the modern synthetic environment, with nature gone and ineffective where it remains, the need for integration and vitalization is acute, and it is just this need that can be met by the highly dynamic imageries of vitalist Abstract Expressionism, imageries capable of symbolizing vitality even more powerfully than nature.

The painter and the critic

As we know him today, the professional critic is a relatively recent product of the rationalization of art at the height of the Age of Reason, and it is on a rationalistic, deterministic, analytical approach to art that he relies. Used to precisions, he can find nothing but contradiction in the new painting, and, trained to look for bridges with the past, he can find none, and so the tendency to dismiss the new as simply not painting at all. At the best, he is equipped by training, attitude, and feeling for going up to the Traditional Modern, but not a step beyond it.

That such a critic still holds a position of often great authority in society today is proof enough that a majority of people are simply not living emotionally in the present at all, and often enough do not even wish to do so, that the age is ravaged by a chronic and insidious escapsim. The new art, to the extent that it is a visible incrimination, is to be blocked, slandered. The word 'artist' has come to mean someone in show business, a revealing cultural indicator. The encouragement of the arts of the past, of unrelated art, not only becomes the most effective blockage to the really new and demanding, but can be played as a game that demands no effort, a game of aesthetic ludo. This playing to avoid the seriousness and demands of becoming involved is a very common trait, part of the modern mechanism of escape. Let us sing and dance and be merry, for we are really dead. In patronizing a dead, meaningless art, the critic placates and pleases the public, in a cynical sense even performs a public duty. It becomes his role, as much as the clown's, to distract from the meaningful, and this he can do all the better under the guise of impartiality and the pomp of savantism.

If one were to make a list of the most significant painters of the nineteenth and early twentieth centuries, one would find that they had all been attacked and vilified by the pontiff critics of the day, and an arousal to violence was advocated on more than one occasion. Yet almost every single one of these critics is now forgotten, proof of their non-involvement in the art that mattered. Today the same thing goes on. The art which is really important in terms of the germinal present is attacked or ignored, and the insignificant praised, flattered. The function of the pontiff critic is, in fact, to defend the established, to put on the brake, to provide what people really require and save them undue effort at readjustment.

The generous support in expensive paper space the pontiff critic gets today not only shows a survival of potent traditionalism and change hating, but a more contorted psychological process. A large number of people, perhaps a majority in a traditionalizing country like England, are suspicious of the new arts, at times of all art. If they feel that they must play some sort of cultural game, none the less they cannot resist opportunities to slash at art. The Press barons, as much as the editors, reveal themselves as a particular type of human being, essentially extroverts—anything less robust would fail to survive in the jungles of a Press office— and the deeply anchored dislike of this type for the introvert is historical; the pontiff critic becomes a means of getting at him, under the cover of fine velvet, and the immunity of the critic from the reply of artists makes the denigration all the more effective. Naturally, none of these subterfuges is fully realized consciously; all happens in the most decent of worlds. But the fact is that in an age crying for really meaningful art, tepid watery soup is served. There are fortunately exceptions, but the mechanism of giving public importance to the pontiff critic and his pronouncements and judgements goes on in the best of the Press.

In a world still largely traditionalized and Renaissance at heart, the pontiff critic is often also called upon to play an even more decisive role in the machinery of celebrity making, by his rulings and advice on selection committees and the attribution of prizes, which usually have a catalytic effect on an artist's reputation. A list of the prizewinners in the national and international arenas shows a virtual exclusion of the advanced painting: it is the Traditional Abstract that wins out nearly every time.

But in spite of such support, the pontiff critic is on the way out. An increasing number of people are not taking him seriously. The committed collectors and dealers ignore him. If the failure of the pontiff critic has offered an opportunity for unequipped and often narrowminded agents, a new yet serious approach to art criticism is becoming essential.

The collapse of traditional art history is not the end of all possible study, of all order. Some notable attempts have been made to relate art to society, to psychology[68] and the possible connexions of art and image with physiology, with biology, in the study of drugs and even of such things as cybernetics, have been mentioned.

The critic need no longer seek infallible guidance, nor need his judgement be his guide. Like and dislike are always personal judgements, and rationalized knowledge makes a man no better for it. What has to be done is to adopt an existential stand. His proper function is to relate, to trace functional connexions with the contemporary scene and the contemporary environment, with the entire situation of modern man, with all aspects of contemporary thought and action, feeling and living, and so to provide art, artists, and art lovers with an essential social and contemporary reference.

The painter and the public

Under all conditions, the products of art are much desired, and the primitive pays as much in his currencies of yams and cowries as the modern magnate. Furthermore, the apparently enormous prices paid for works of art today are not that much more than a century ago if inflation is reckoned with.[69]

Good historical art is bound to get ever scarcer, as world population and prosperity increases.

Prosperous communities as much as wealthy individuals are usually materialistic, and if this helps in a ruthlessly competitive capitalistic world, it is deadly to the soul. And the soul will not die lightly and reacts by crying out from the depths for aid. Art is the one purchasable fruit of the deep spirit, the one procurable prophylactic against spiritual necrosis. So it is that the rising new cities and states as much as the lucred magnate must have their own soul-saving collection, and that must mean not only more art, and higher-priced historical art, but more dealers and dealing.

It is a common misconception that rich people only buy art for speculation; conditioned as they are to the money value of things, one cannot blame them for applying such values also to art, but as one comes to know them one finds that they love their collections. Art has such hypnotic and converting powers that even if one were to begin a collection for purely venal reasons, then one would become converted to a genuine love in time, and this remark applies even to the dealer; one has to go a very long way to find one of any time and experience not deeply involved in the aesthetics of his profession.

Although much publicity is given in the Press to the buying antics of the very rich—no one really likes very rich people—the biggest factor in price fixing today is the professional buyer. If the socialistically minded person, disgusted by this stampede in art as a commodity, looks to an end of it in the triumph of world socialism, he is likely to be proved wrong. The USSR have kept their moderns and are discreetly hanging them; with an inevitable growing in the freedom of taste, there is going to be a very big call there and an enormous gap of half a century of neglect to fill. The proud peoples of Azerbaijan will also want their museums up to date and in the glorious art traditions of the Russian past, one of the first great leaders in the rise of the moderns. As it is, tolerated activities or clandestine explorations into the abstract are rife, and one even hears of private collectors in Soviet Russia.

But, as one must expect, there is a contradiction to this somewhat simple-minded acceptance of the money-value of art. This money-valuation is in reality a transference of a system of appraisal that belongs to other objects, objects that properly belong to the realm of material exchanges, of things that can be ordered and paid for by measure and weight. The real value of art is an anarchical value, one that precisely is above such a common evaluation. In any proper system, art should, at least in theory, be able to scorn the valuation of money and ride on a higher plane, one in which there is no barter and bargaining, no corruption. Art, in fact, should be beyond price. As Hannah Arendt says, in any system of exchanges, it is necessary to have 'objects which are strictly without any utility whatsoever and which, moreover, because they are unique, are not exchangeable and therefore defy equalization through a common denominator such as money'—art. Permanence necessarily becomes a requirement of such objects.

From this standpoint the most valuable art should be the most worthless aesthetically, and the most worthless might well be the most valid in that it is the defiance of money-valuation. It is probably true that any genuine artist, if he could be assured of a living, would welcome the exclusion of his art from the commercial stampede of commercial art dealing, and many an artist, if only from time to time, rebels, and ensures that his art becomes an anarchical defiance of the commercial bond, if only by destroying it, or monstrously offending the established codes of dealers.

Compromise is nearly a dirty word, but the mind has to compromise with matter at every step, in every undertaking. If the commercialization of art is inevitable, and as such must be accepted existentially, it remains none the less the role of the artist to remember and constantly refresh his rebellious attitude to it.

If only pitiable sums are made available officially in England,[70] in other countries the official appropriation is generous. In France and Germany architects are encouraged to provide a percentage of costs for works of art: in France it is compulsory. In the big buildings of today even a fraction of one per cent would amount to a generous patronage. There are also concessions in some countries which enable the cost of purchase of works of art to be deducted from tax by private individuals.

This ever-increasing pressure of demand has inevitably encouraged the professional fakers. There are now well-known methods whereby competent fakes can be 'assimilated' into the respectable ranks of the loved and eternal ones. Once assimilated, with known collectors and a sufficient pedigree behind them, the fakes are as good as genuine, and there are collectors who have bought such fakes knowingly, protected by an elaborate professional backing. And as for the unknown fakes, they are legion, but with an internationally organized ring it is becoming impossible for the small-time faker to break in; it is an exclusive business. It is true that suspicion now is more often aroused by a painting which is too good than by a clumsy one. There can be no doubt, for instance, that Van Meegeren's Christ at Emmaus is superlative Vermeer.[71]

What has so far been said applies particularly to historical art,

art which is already widely accepted, and which is on the line of cultural development. Although not contemporarily valid, such art must necessarily be collected and treasured by the community for a variety of reasons. It is this line of development that decides the pricing of any historical piece; any offshoots are always less highly priced, and it is the art which is outside this line which can fall, often sensationally, never the art on the historical line. While European art was reacting to the rising industrial age in Impressionism and all that followed it, another branch of European art went along blindly the way of Renaissance realism into a dead end of mimetic and sentimental insignificance, and it is this that has fallen. A portrait by some socially popular portraitist of today, costing perhaps as much as £2,000, may be worthless in a couple of decades or less.

Today it is fairly clear how this line runs, and the big-money collector is likely to reserve his activities to it, from the tremblings of the Impressionists to the Traditional Modern. There is such a thing as a 'natural history' of art dealing, as every dealer knows. Dealers may make errors of timing, the most common being to stick at the period of their youthful loves, but all the successful ones have an implicit faith in such a natural history. Talk of fashion and unrelated changes does not worry them, for fashion, although it may seem enormously important for a short present, has little to do with the longer runs of the story of art collection and values.

It is a certain fact that time will judge an artist alive today, in the new painting as much as in the Traditional Modern, by the time of his entry and contribution. A later entry, in some ways almost certainly plagiaristic, is bound to be worth much less on every count than one who was at the front, even if he made no particular contribution. This observation only applies to the time of great change or revolution; and it is likely to be much less important in the subsequent variations and mutations. Already today the very young are outside it; in a true sense, it matters much less what they do.

At present big pressure promotion is still chiefly concerned with the Traditional Moderns, but ever more dealers are taking up the new painting. The prices of some of the key Americans are soaring. The new dealers are in many respects quite different from the established dealers. The nineteenth-century dealer was something of a dilettante, advising his client broadly, impartially. This kind of big-eyed dealer is on the way out and is being replaced by a growing number of 'committed dealers' who deal at the most with a few painters and devote all their time and resources to them.

The promotion of the new painting only involves a relatively few lucky artists. Today there are others who are working along significant lines, but who are not 'in' and can be bought cheaply. The big promotion business is not by any means entirely under professional control; quite unpredictable things can happen, the great can suddenly fall, whispering campaigns can wreck the best reputations, and quite suddenly a relatively unknown name can rocket up. But if what the collector of the 'out' artists collects is on the line of significance, then, sooner or later, his collection is bound to increase in value. If the diagnosis contained in this book is at all correct, the chances of buying the new paintings today very cheaply and seeing them soar in the future are still there. As the new painting comes to be seen as the real painting of the times, prices will begin the same rocketing that has gone on with the Impressionists and Traditional Abstracts. But faith is required and much patience.

And the situation is admittedly confusing for the collector, with numerous distractions and false claims around him. Although in the long run fashion is irrelevant, in the short run it can easily deceive. An example is provided by the recent revivals of 'hard edge' and of geometric imageries of one kind and another in England and America, a revival that has received considerable backing from critics, architects and intellectuals for a variety of reasons (see pp. 17, 94).

There are even more distracting influences at work. Some artists, sensing that they have run up the wrong line and desperate to make some claim to originality, look around for some appearance of novelty, for some entry into the abstract field. This is easy enough to find in the junk heaps of experiment which all genuine artists continually indulge in, and the imageries of the Traditional Modern period can easily be trumped up to look like something new. This is crassly dishonest, and it is bound to be found out in time, but the unwary collector and even the critic can be duped.

One of the more evil aspects of fashion is the clamour for endless change, and here the collector is as much to blame as the dealer. Most people have come to look upon change as a part of life. But if the argument of this book is valid and art is related to environmental change, the last great and basic revolution is probably over. Dalliance is henceforth a symptom of superficiality, not of genius; or of forced acrobatics which is worse. There will no doubt be endless alterations and mutations around the prototypes, but that is something different.

Much clearer thinking is required as to the meaning of terms like the new, like change and progress in matters of art. Alteration is continuous and can be followed from stage to stage, whereas original creation is entirely without precedent. This is illustrated in biology. Truly original features in animals and plants occur in sudden and unpredictable jumps or mutations, whereas most of evolution consists of progressive changes working upon these sudden and often unwelcome apparitions. So in art, truly great and original creations are as untraceable and original and although it is a human tendency to look for traces and antecedents—it is the bread-and-butter of the critic—only small fluff can be found in this way. But the bulk of art history *is* change and alteration and can afford browsing-ground to the art historian—unfortunately, it is the least important aspect of it.

Anyway, the notion of progress in art is entirely misplaced. As Cassirer points out, although it is valid in the logical order of things, in art 'we are confronted, not with a peaceful development of concepts and theories, but with a clash between conflicting powers . . . fraught with the deepest human passions'. It is the transposition of ideas of progress, of novelty and perfection which apply in the common realms of human endeavour to art which is at fault, the error of a deterministic age. An art which was moving to perfection would have need of imperfection.

The young are particularly subject to corruption by this false priority on novelty. They are by nature and character more likely to change, and the young painter today is often in a quandary. With the pressure of fashion, and sensing that all has none the less already been done, he is apt rush to off in frenzies of flourish and recipe hunting. One finds young painters trying anything, everything, and ransacking the garbage for originality at any cost. Under such conditions it is probably true that the better bet for a collector is not the young but the maturing artist.

But perhaps the biggest danger is the lack of a sufficient appreciation of the importance of what an artist does and when he does it. There is a 'Natural History' of the new also. The worst sort of buy today is likely to turn out to be the artist who has made his name in some sort of compromised realism and comes late into the abstract field just because it is felt belatedly to be the thing to do. One sees this happening all around one, and a previous reputation makes the public take to them with greater confidence. This is especially so in the English scene, where there is a poor appreciation of the value of timing, owing to the unfortunate fact that England has played no part in the rise of modern painting; critics, dealers, and collectors tend to take it as a virtue that a particular painter has been through the 'traditional mill' and only later gone abstract—how late does not seem to matter to them—and in ways long since pioneered and staked, which time is bound to dishonour.

Only a few years ago it was being prophesied that the private purchaser of paintings was to be superseded by 'social' art. Today one finds the commercial galleries full and much of the buying is done by quite ordinary people, who would never think of themselves as big-time collectors. There are no doubt many explanations of this fact, but surely the most pertinent is that it is a human prerogative to choose and select, to make one's mark against the passage of time by emotional choice and commitment, and that an increasingly prosperous community is bound to exercise this right to an increasing extent. It is an observable fact that only the very big collectors allow themselves to be advised on matters of purchase: to most people it is the choosing, right or wrong, which is a good part of the pleasure.

This is something one can never get from a visit to a public gallery, and for the gallery to attempt to rival the intimate and personal function of art is absurd. Yet this is just what it tries often to do today, to do no more than show people paintings. This anomaly is a survival of the traditional function of the gallery and museum, when the painting was in truth a 'piece of reality' and as many pieces as possible could be shown legitimately; all people had to do was to look. Today, with the new paintings, this kind of presentation is apt to be confusing and misleading. The painting, it has been emphasized, is not just a caught moment of something else; it is a thing in itself, and tends to occupy its entire environment by the symbolic radiation of its energies and tensions. Its environment is a part of it, and a most essential one at that (see p. 80). It follows therefore that the painting cannot be simply hung virtually anywhere and as many as will go. If there are to be 'social' or 'public' paintings, and indeed there must be, then they are not to be hung after the spaces are done, but they should be thought of in terms of the entire space and environment creatively.

It is not so much a question of 'living with the painting', but of the painting being able to live with its surroundings and so perform its full and unimpeded emotional job of restoration and radiation. Then it can but be a part of one'a life.

Along some such lines, the public gallery awaits its revolution. To put several paintings in one room, often in contrary appeal, is to invite emotional cancellation and confusion. The 'big room' is a Renaissance survival, although sufficient space is required for the new paintings to work out. The more symbolically dynamic, then the more space is needed. Some of the most dynamic paintings of our time would need virtually an entire room to themselves. There are also possibilities of mechanization, arrangements for paintings to be changed at regular intervals, or possibly in certain cases changed by the spectator.

Attempts are being made to put the print over as an answer to the expensive painting, and the way of making art 'democratic'. Yet the print's smooth, precise qualities fit it ideally to a traditional imagery, and if it can still suit a Traditional Modern image, it lacks some of the essential 'matter' and spontaneity, qualities of the valid painting of today. It would be far better for artists to make monochrome rubbings, sketches, and rough calligraphies. The better among them can then be picked out. The limitations on drawing and the sketch are fully appreciated today, but such rough calligraphic expressions, much easier than a painting, can often retain the artist's stamp and are strictly unique.

It is also possible for the artist to make several examples near enough to some especially picked original, which can be numbered as in a series and sold more cheaply. This suggestion will seem outrageous to the traditionally minded, with his ideas of the uniqueness of art and the degradation of every copy, but a strict copying is not involved. It is rather the circumnavigation of a theme, which is an essential part of many techniques today. Many artists do as a matter of course paint several paintings together, in order to reduce conscious choices as to colour, to allow some theme to work itself out, and to have a wider choice for post-creative selection. This is implicit in the opportunistic, experimental approach of the new painting. So, with the rapid calligraphies or washes suggested, copying could bring out latent possibilities not realized in the original, and varying with each attempt. Repetition here is neither mimetic nor is it mechanical. It is a development of the image as part of a process; as the living organism, repetitive and yet unique, is part of the stream of life and of evolution, and like life, the more one does, then the more there is mutation, alteration.

9

PAINTING AND THE OTHER ARTS

The key position of painting

ALL artistic expression is the symbolic actualization of an underlying emotionalism which is at the heart of all human thought,
vision, feeling, and action. Although reason will not
give it much due, this basic emotionalism is elaborately organized
and perfected as the emotional inner world of man, which has not
only an order of its own, allowing for endless flux and change, but
a 'life' of its own also. It appears to be always running, even when
there are no images to it, even when it is remembered by the
conscious mind by no more than vague moods and inexplicable
feelings. Its aspects are by their very nature in ceaseless alteration,
and it is this ceaselessness that makes the human mind pounce so
avidly upon every and any external situation capable of symbolic
interpretation in order to have some stake in space and time. And
virtually *any* external object or scene can serve such an end, in some
way peculiar to itself, uniquely symbolic.

The different arts merely provide different opportunities for
particular aspects of the emotional psyche to manifest and exercise
itself, and one finds that each art has a distinct symbolic individuality that cannot be properly provided by any other art. So if all
the arts serve some underlying common emotional function, they
are also distinct and individual.

Since the emotional order of the mind is fundamentally different
from the external physical order, any appearance of interfusion
between the two is only illusional. The symbolically freest art
is likely to be the one to do best and most complete service
to the inner emotional world, and it is in this sense that music
has been timelessly considered the 'highest' art. Music can, in
fact, be enjoyed in a pure symbolic emotionalism, without any
visual or other reminders of the external order. It is art in
its purest form. Realist art, and literature, are on the other

hand conditioned to considerable degrees by the necessity of making the emotional current run close to external requirements. In drama, in poetry, in ballet, a greater measure of detachment becomes possible. Painting today has, however, gone as far as music in being able to deal with a quite disembodied symbolization of emotion, and the privileged position of music in the arts no longer applies.

Since classical music developed a near mathematical preciseness and deterministic symbolism, a much freer painting today has a considerable advantage. Ambiguity in music is foreign to the entire Western tradition, though one does find instances of it in the music of other cultures and of primitives the world over. And music has the disadvantage, today in process of being corrected by electronics, of having to be performed, and poetry is best read and competently read at that, whereas a painting is always there, available for emotional reference and guidance at any time.

So it is that painting today, even more than a groping music struggling to find the ways and means out of an ancient determinism, has become well equipped for symbolizing the emotional reactions of the age in their most free and yet evident manner. Painting, rather than music has become the yardstick for the comparison of the validty of the other arts which are less free and more interefered with by non-aesthetic influences. If Goethe compared classical architecture to frozen classical music—a very apt comparison—the comparison breaks down today. If one wishes to find the symbolic validity of any human activity today, he would do best to go to painting, for here are all the essentials of symbolic validity in their most evident and articulate forms.

Architecture

The importance of architecture comes from the fact that the architectonic qualities of the new, man-made environment are overwhelmingly predominant, and that if the supreme and ultimate challenge facing a humanity that has dispensed with nature is to find ways and means of emotionalizing and thus of humanly reclaiming the environment, architecture should play a leading role in this achievement.

In contrast to painting and sculpture, which are entirely made for aesthetic communication, all the other visual things which are man-made, including buildings, have a practical obligation. In machines, the practical needs totally exclude any imposed aesthetic expression. In less functionally exacting things, such as kitchen gadgets, practical considerations still predominate, but visual appeals can be modified without interfering with functional intentions so as to provide a superimposed aesthetic contribution. In still less pragmatically demanding things, such as a radio set, the aesthetic contribution can be so big as to decide the entire visual, symbolic aspect, and intended visual and tactile gratification can form an important feature of such things.

The case of architecture is somewhat special. It is essential that definite practical criteria be met—living and working space—but to some extent these requirements are elastic and can be modified for aesthetic ends; the degree of modification or formal conditioning will depend on whether or not an aesthetic modification can be absorbed without adding to the cost, or, if an additional cost is involved, to what degree the client or the community is prepared to go to meet the cost, and only then does the question of the architect's ability to be an expressive artist really arise.

The cheapest means of providing space is cubistic, and any deviation from a simple geometry for purely aesthetic ends must cost more, so that the only aesthetics which architecture can provide directly today and without any extra cost is a rectilinear or tubular architecture and a relatively simple geometric aesthetics. The first question that one must therefore ask is whether such a cubistic architecture can constitute valid art today.

No one would wish to deny that architecture has produced great works of art in the past, valid in its time and place, and the imposed aesthetic contribution has at times been considerable, in a Gothic cathedral, in an Indian temple, in a Venetian Palazzo. Form here is definitely manipulated, used expressively, emotionally, which is art. Conditions then were quite different from the present, both emotionally and practically. Emotionally, in Europe anyway, classical, deterministic ideals prevailed, and thus are ideally met by some sort of geometric imagery, and the practical requirements of space were certainly much less exacting. Often sponsored by privileged and wealthy classes, by lavish courts, or by wealthy patrons like the Church, emotional factors were frequently more important than purely practical ones, the urges for display, for propaganda, for self or celestial vindication or for sheer exuberance ending in the 'folly mentality', the kind of flourish which only the devout or the idle rich can afford or have time for. So the simple geometrisms of practical structure became elaborated by extravagant and costly modulations, so that even in the Age of Reason, when precise, deterministic criteria prevailed and could have found adequate emotional fulfilment in a precise, deterministic architecture, even then we find that this architecture is variously flourished and rendered more symbolically complex.

But since the Industrial Revolution economic factors have been almost entirely decisive; in an age crying for housing and working space any other provision becomes impermissible. And so architecture has become ever more cubistic, simply geometric in its emotional impacts, a trend that has been further enforced by architects themselves, influenced by a misguided functional aesthetics.[72] Misguided, for such a simple geometric image, from all that has been said already (p. 89), can but provide a traditional, classical image, quite out of line with the valid feelings and emotional requirements of the times.

There have been reactions within architecture against this, for instance in brutalism, but so strong is the geometric impact, dictated by pragmatic forces today, that a little uncouthness here or there does not overcome the overall geometric, classical, purist impact. The belief in the effectiveness of brutalism has existed largely in architects' minds, as an intellectual affair, rather than in practice. And it could anyway only be a natural brutalism, one coming from the unfinish of materials themselves. As soon as it tries to become more, and becomes calculated and intended, it is contrived adornment which is immediately rejectable aesthetically.

The question then becomes: Can architecture today be an expressive art, or is it to be considered as simply a practical affair, providing in its course an aesthetics which is out of time and place and which can therefore be disregarded?

An artist or sculptor can have hand-to-eye control over his materials so that intuited guidance and choice are close. If he fails to wield his materials to emotional effect, he can summarily discard the result and start again without the community being in any way punished. And among the best artists, at all times there has been a considerable crop of inevitable failures. Architecture is not only spatially extensive, and so direct emotional control over its materials becomes incomparably more difficult, but it is

136

time-enduring, and, up to now, few have thought of making an architecture than could be modified and altered and adjusted, in the way that, in fact, every artist operates.

So even with the best architects, acting as artists, one must expect a very high proportion of failures, and this means not only paying for an expressive largesse which surely only a community that has solved all its practical needs should afford on any socio-logical morality, but it means living with the failures—or destroy-ing them.

It might be contended that the architect, in his planning and in his models, can reduce this added risk of total emotional failure, by selecting the most aesthetic choices. But this would only be true if scale did not come into emotional choices—and we are at present only talking of emotional ones, which are different by nature from practical ones. The entire spectrum of emotion is affected by scale; a miniature painting, though similar in every respect to a large painting, will have quite a different meaning in art, and as every painter who has tried a really big painting without sufficient emotional drive will know, the 'blow-up' is about the greatest disaster one can have, emotionally. It is not simply dilution; it is vacuous failure. Art, to be art, is entirely decided by actual, actualized symbols which cannot be transposed, inflated, or reduced without entire symbolic alteration. The error comes from imagining intellectually that this is possible.

It is true that many a plan, on the drawing-board, has an 'organic' and often valid look about it, but the satisfaction to be got from such a contemplation is quite academic. It is entirely lost in the practical execution, and plans which seemed most exciting come out as eternal variants of that same bland geometrism at the human level. There is little doubt that the attractions of the drawing-board, among many dreamy-eyed architects and intro-verts, explain a frequent concomitant distrust of practical realiza-tion of their work. They know that in some way it is bound to be a let-down.

So the risk of great failure remains, and when the adulation of the architect-autocrats like Le Corbusier dies down, the crop of failures will become all too evident. Although in such a confused subject as architecture hero worship is inevitable, the failures are becoming already apparent. Only a very extravagant age could afford such a hit-or-miss architecture, in its most indestructible form, an indestructibility itself unnecessary and an aspect of the 'classical complex'.

And even when such expressive latitude is granted to the architect, the validity of the resulting imagery remains to be questioned. Convoluted and altered, massive or slimmed, the emotional impact most usually remains of the geometric order, and remains classical in feeling as so much of Le Corbusier's work happens to be.

It can be seen that it is the underlying vision, the emotional character-type of architects as well as the pragmatic restriction of the times that is at work. Even if given the chance of expression, they do little more than offer the traditional geometric image. If, however, this background of architectural feeling could, in fact, be changed, there might well be found possibilities of providing a more valid image in architecture within economic bounds, or at least if they are exceeded, one could be better assured of a valid expenditure.

The main impediment at present is the personality type of the architect today, trained, and probably selected by temperament and ability, to have a somewhat puritanical cubistic constitution in matters of taste, to prefer simplicity to ambiguity, geometric precision to any of its possible alternatives. In the past, and, of course, in a straightforward pragmatic commercial architecture, these are indeed essential qualities for success. But a pursuit of simplicity, we have seen, is a classical pursuit, and bound to end in a classical statement.

Such things as traffic, at present largely ignored emotionally, could be made to provide a considerable degree of dynamism to the architectural scene, and things like lifts, now meticulously enclosed—one of the most inhuman aspects of modern archi-tecture, since some 28 per cent of people have claustrophobic symptoms—and essential machines could bring in many elusive and dynamic symbols. Circularities, webbings, flutings which can now be made easily by pressings and moulds, especially with new materials like plastics, vaultings and crisscrossings of structure could provide an enormous symbolic wealth and a measure of visual ambiguity essential if the impact is to be valid and con-temporary.

As already emphasized, it does not matter if the result is obtained by calculation: it is the symbolic judgement that finally counts (p. 93). This does not imply unnecessary complexity, which also becomes adornment and is aesthetically rejectable: it means functional complexity. At present, thanks to his training and outlook, the architect simplifies by reflex. He could produce a much more valid result by an opposite respect of potential complexity and to build around it, much more demanding no doubt, but about the only way out.

An attitude more compatible with complex situations could also provide buildings which would be capable of adjustment, of growth in pluridimension, of contraction.[73] In such an archi-tectural milieu, the many possibilities of surface modulation would have a chance of working, the uses of variable light, the organized reflections of sky, cloud and water on shining surfaces and texture-gradation could all contribute towards a valid imagery in architecture. The idea of an expendable architecture has barely been entertained—the idea that buildings might be built to be rejected after a relatively short period of time rather than made enduring, a possibility well within the practical means of realiza-tion today with plastic mouldings. One can see that the idea of endurance, as in industry and no doubt in art itself, is symptomatic of the classical mind, of its belief in finality, in constancy and resistance to change and alteration. Yet an expendable architecture would not only make for a more rich and variable life and environ-ment, but would fit in with the emotion of the age.

But architects being what they are, by training and no doubt by constitution and psychology, only a revolution could bring about the state of mind that would take such suggestions seriously and take on the research and experiment which would be essential. Far more likely, architecture will continue in its present cubisms, providing the required spaces in the cheapest of ways, but nothing else.

The fact that such a cubistic architecture is emotionally invalid today can be found in the common disregard of such buildings by the people who have to live in and around them: the only satisfac-tion belongs to the architect, and it is a purely intellectual one. Glass box architecture is just neutral architecture; people are not even aware of it emotionally. This is truly an appalling state of affairs, and amounts to an environment bereft of human and humanizing meaning.

At a purely existential level the only possible answer is for this neutral architecture to be given emotional meaning by an inclusion of valid works of art. Here one meets with an immediate doctrinal objection from the architect. The Beaux Arts attitude has encouraged the belief that the architectural surface and space are sacrosanct, complete and entire in themselves, and any suggestion of artistic collaboration to supply a full human spectrum of emotion singularly neglected by architecture is seen as interference.

It is not the adding of a sculpture here and a painting there that is suggested. At the conceptual stage the architect should be able to envisage the co-operation of the artist's contribution. The architect, while providing the spaces pragmatically, and thus in no way an expressive artist, would yet require the wisdom, sensitivity, education and high culture to be able to see beyond this and to integrate an entire cultural sensibility into the environment. That there are some big-minded architects today who strive to do just this is most encouraging, but the architectural bigot also abounds and tends to settle in the intellectual positions of power which have far more influence than they merit. A new *élite* in architecture is as necessary as anywhere else, and active on all its fronts, in architectural journalism, in architectural research and teaching as in actual design.

Unfortunately, one is here up against psychological incompatibility. Architectural commercial success today can only come from a pragmatic, cubistic type of mind, and the combination of this with the more intellectual Beaux Arts classicism of architectural education makes for a narrow-gauge product. To such a mind, the most compatible image is most likely to be some sort of 'hard edge' constructivism. The more free the image, the more he will tend to react against it, instinctively, and the tendency to reject or ignore the kind of valid paintings described in this book will be *plus fort que lui*. Only a drastic revolution in architectural education and a widening of subjects taught, and the putting of architecture on a dynamic experimental basis, is likely to make co-operation between the architect and the artist more than an exceptional possibility.

What a neutral architecture will have to do is to provide the full emotional spectrum of appeal which human beings require, which they once obtained from nature, and which now they must obtain in synthetic works of art. Roughly, this means providing for two opposite appeals, the 'energetic' and the 'quietist'; examples of both these kinds of imageries have already been given. An architecture that itself can manage to provide some measure of a more complex, ambiguous, and dynamic appeal, as suggested above, can meet some of the needs, although great scope is certain to remain for a more specific art contribution. What a neutral, cubistic architecture is certain to fail to provide, except to the extent that it can make use of such things as traffic, people, machinery, and of light, is a sufficient energetic contribution. And it is this that the human being requires most pressingly in an age and environment which is not only unvital, but antivital.

In order to get some sort of idea as to the proportion of 'energetic' and 'quietist' appeals from the environment that would suit human beings best one can do no better than consider the proportion of these in a normal, natural environment. Although human beings are widely adaptable to the most varied environments, it is more than likely that the human species was created in a fairly specific environment, in a 'naturalistic' nature, in fact (p. 7). In such an environment 'quietist' appeals are diffuse and discreet, consisting of such things as the sky, water, the inter-harmony of things, the soft line of the land, whereas dynamic, energetic, vitalistic appeals are predominant and often striking, in the constant changes in all things, in the weather, in diurnal variations, in the seasons, in the growth and movement of living things. Nature throbs and pulsates, a pulsation which is in every part of our being, in the beat of our hearts as in the Berger rhythms of our brain, and in all human arts, especially music. It is difficult to guess at this preponderance, but it is probably in the neighbourhood of 60 to 80 per cent of the total emotional impact.

When this proportion falls, then human beings react in many ways to replace the decreasing vitality, in music and dance, in violent behaviour, in energetic art, all evident today. It might be contended that modern life does provide in its reactions and in its restlessness an overabundance already of energetic symbols. Unfortunately, the bulk of this is disorganized, disjointed, disturbing (p. 57). *In nature, the energizing symbols are always associated with order and harmony.* In the energetic expressions of other cultures, of primitives, in such things as communal dances and ceremonies, even in war-preparing and war-waging activities, elaborate order and ritual are observed,[74] whereas many of our equivalent activities today are wantonly Dionysian and disorderly. So the modern environment on its own cannot make a contribution to the needs of energetic symbolization. This can only come from an energetic art; hence its pivotal importance today.

Some day architecture may well be able to take on more directly a good part of the human expressive needs, and so become itself an expressive art. Uses of atomic energy and plastics may in time give great expressive elasticity to architecture, but even then, if such an architecture could no doubt go a long way in dispensing with sculpture, specific contributions of the flat image would remain. It will be recalled that a painting is flat not because it cannot be three-dimensional (p. 91), but because flatness in itself has an immense symbolic power, and a flat image has a function that no three-dimensional image could ever satisfy. So the sympathy which many architects feel for sculpture is the prelude to an eventual cannibalism, but the most distant architecture will still have to reckon with painters as separate creators, as providers of a unique symbolic food—if they are to meet all human emotional requirements. They might as well learn to make proper use of them.

It is not necessary for such a future architecture to go the way of rococo and of Gaudi. There is among the present valid imageries of painting a 'soft edge' as well as a tense, turgid expressionistic structure which are more likely to be prophetic of future architectural feeling. An 'action architecture' or an 'architectural tachisme' is absurd. But it is as yet impossible to say how architectural shape will go; it will depend largely on concepts of the city which have still to be worked out. Will the cities of the future be vast organized sprawls, or will they be compact and multiple nucleations like cells joined by neurons over the countryside, itself then largely become neutral, or will cities be more transient, expendable things, or will they be limited to the face of the land or soar into the clouds floating or into the depths of the oceans? But one thing is likely, a growing complexity will, poetically speaking, produce a city more like the human body than the pile of varied shoeboxes of the present day.

And when all is said and done, we may be asking too much of any human being in the guise of even the most superlative architects. The best brain has its limits, and the co-ordination and correlation of data which the overall integration of the human environment will demand may well overstep its limits. There can be little doubt that the computer will be called in to help, and a far more dynamically minded architecture come round to solving many of its problems in an experimental manner like any other creative challenge: there are all the advantages of exteriorizing choice, selection and rejection, which is all that the experiment is, and if technologists have found this essential for dealing with practical matters, it is obvious that architecture, in its practical aspects, should take good heed of this approach.

It is also possible that computers yet to be designed will be able to take note of both the deterministic and the analogical, and so will be able to help in more than the purely pragmatic challenges of architecture, helping to correlate and fuse together both the practical and the emotional. If the suggestion that such a computer could provide the means of building an entire city starting from a scanned piece of sculpture and properly encoded pragmatic requirements, would today draw nothing but smiles, it may well be possible some day, in the perfect balancing of the pragmatic and the emotional in forms that no human mind could predict.

Sculpture

An object in three dimensions naturally symbolizes external reality, and the primitive visions lurking in the depths of the human mind, a 'black and white' vision, spooky, hairy, spiky, and often obscene and demonic, the 'geometry of fear' as Sir Herbert Read put it. So that if sculpture leaves the visible world of ready appearances, it is most likely to go either this way or the way of geometry, still thoroughly external in feeling. Almost all so-called modern sculpture belongs to the traditional, classical, or primitive space relationships. Perhaps the only way three-dimensional forms have managed to break into a new range of feeling, equivalent to the new painting, is in machines and in moving structures like those of Schoeffer's 'spatiodynamic' pieces which even incorporate moving lights and sounds.

In its three-dimensionality, sculpture belongs to the 'black and white' vision which existed before the emergence of colour in human evolution. It is not that sculpture cannot transcend this 'primitive' heritage of its shapes, forms, and spaces; it can do so magnificently, but none the less some ancestral colour and form incompatibility remains. The Greek artists did not colour their sculpture themselves; the colour was a non-aesthetic ritualistic or decorative imposition made in the temple or precinct by priests or decorators. No great coloured sculpture exists: coloured objects acquire an emotional quality that makes them quite different from sculpture. Not only the emotional, but the physiological processes of colour and form vision are separate and quite different within the retina and probably within the brain. The common preoccupation of sculptors to paint, or of painters to sculpt today is a symptom of the restless groping for new and different expression. The mechanisms are too opposite to be capable of being fully articulate in one and the same person. They are the denial of each other.

Music and ballet

Melody is the equivalent of those visual cues in nature which elicit the humanizing emotions, and melody has suffered much the same fate of scrambling as nature in painting. The scrambling in composers like Schoenberg remains discernibly 'naturalistic', and this kind of music still belongs in a camouflaged way to the traditional, like the Traditional Modern in painting. The new music comes with Webern and only a sprinkling of others, the late Stravinsky, Stockhausen, Boulez, Chauvez, Badings and the 'synthetic composers'.[75] Jazz is in good part still traditional, although its use of the beat and of most complex rhythms has a dismembering effect upon melody and tends to counter its 'naturalism'.

Indeterminism and ambiguity are being introduced into music in a variety of ways; by structural 'opacity', as it was in fugal pre-Renaissance music which can often feel very 'modern' emotionally—and by the microdissection of sound as in a free serialism. A freedom of execution is also explored, as in Stockhausen and in the 'jam sessions' of jazz. Although still in the laboratory stage, this music is coming to take a functional and closely related part in daily life in the post-atomic age; it is its own music, now being used in advertising, in films, in ballet, and as a background to such things as flight and space project reports. In time, it may well become built-in in various ways with the environment and so produce the background of sound essential to human welfare (p. 48).

Ballet, like sculpture, is figuratively handicapped, but experiments are going on, even in Communist countries,[76] in an attempt to use the human body and its movements in a freer symbolism. Although the human face and body shared with certain aspects of nature as the first 'work of art' (p. 3), the fact that the human being is the centre of all feeling—nature is after all always 'something outside'—means that it is possible for the human form to be transcended and dissociated from its naturalistic associations and so to symbolize quite 'synthetic' reactions which man may happen to feel existentially. The phantasmagoria of world-wide dance proves this point. One finds the same thing going on to some extent in athletics, and in the modern theatre. It might be said that man in his every motion and glance has the ability to defy nature, and in a nature-defying environment this becomes all the more evident and possible.

Poetry and literature

Poets and writers such as Ruskin, Coventry Patmore, Matthew Arnold, and later Pound and Eliot, were expanding the free symbolism of traditional writing methods at the same time that the Impressionisists were scrambling visible nature. The ability of writing, even of poetry, to move into an entirely synthetic order of expression is evidently limited: nonsense writing is almost entirely nonsensical. But the remarkable ability of writing to fuse a symbolic with a realistic core does enable it to break through into a new emotional order of experience which no realistic art appears able to do: and this, no doubt because the intellectual imaginability of a scene, is always more ambiguous and potentially free (p. 31) than the visual transcription of it, which is what goes into realistic painting. Great writing wields a special order of 'thisness' and 'otherness', impossible in any realist painting.

New methods have appeared in writing that enhance this effect, in allusive shifts of structure, in allegory and parable, in clashing, startling, juxtaposed meanings pioneered by Surrealism in poetry, and in ambiguities of entire sentences and passages which one finds in Eliot, Dylan Thomas, Pound, Beckett, Ionesco, Pinter, Albee, Simpson, Genet and Kopit. In recent developments in novel writing on the Continent, ambiguity is obtained by a forthright improvization and disdain of deterministic structure.[77]

Curiously enough, prose writing has fared better than poetry in this pursuit, perhaps because of its ability to fuse a strong realistic order in a paradoxical play with symbolic shifts, whereas poetry has strong lyrical strains which have better fitted it to explore the lyricism of nature. One does find that Surrealist poetry passes over into a structure and order closer to writing as it increases in power.

The relevance of this process to painting is that intuitive writings about and around it, lectures and conversations, can have a synergic effect on the painting, on opening up its meaning and enabling a greater receptivity to it, by a quickening of the emotional stream, just as music can do. Although some sort of literal content is necessary for the mind to take in such writing at all, it is not so much this as its intuited symbolisms that really work, and it is no doubt because of this that some of the most inspiring writing on art today has come not from professional art historians but from poets and even from artists themselves.

Design

Every object created by man is an extension of mind and body, and this is as true for a corkscrew as it is for the greatest work of art. A future is likely to judge us as much by the shapes of our cars as by our art.

Only the more dynamic objects are automatically aesthetized; in all other objects, scope for emotional expressive intervention exists, the 'design factor'. At present the attitude to design is largely negative and unco-ordinated; things are made as isolated entities rather than as parts of an entire and mutually influencing environment, whimsy and fashion prevail, and there is a prevalent notion that the designer need not be a particularly good artist. As with architecture, the new painting can act as a yardstick of emotional needs: a comparison of the emotional beam of any object with that of the valid paintings of today can give some idea of the design success or failure of it.

Particularly the superficial attitude to design needs correction. Like any art, design rests on solid genetic foundations. Trinkets, flowers, beads, and ornaments were offered from the earliest days of human courtship by the male to the female as the instinctive evidence of emotional fitness, a form of sex display particular to the human species and still going on, and it is on such symbolic evidence that the female judges instinctively the 'fitness' of her intending mate, for emotional aptness is the equivalent of procreative compatibility (p. 3), a process, incidentally, which is recapitulated in the emotional androgyny of every individual, male *or* female. Body markings, ornaments, hair arrangements, and later clothes and jewellery play their emotionalizing part in this process. It is a complete misjudgement to see human dress and adornment as a copulatory allurement; its most ancient role is just the opposite, the woman's means of emotionalizing sex, of making it expand into an emotionalized union. It has been rightly said that clothes are made by men for women, just as flowers are offered as a symbolic gift of courtship-fitness, and the trades that depend on these functions rest on a very firm biological basis that will go well beyond 1984. As is human, there are endless adaptations, and the fur coat becomes the ice-age offering just as a tender piece of human gastrocnemius is the choice offering among cannibals, but the intention is always worthy.

The trend for emotional sex differences to become levelled down with civilization has already been mentioned (p. 66). The emotional androgyny becomes more active in every person. Clothes can be the most visible signals of sexual demarcation, and we are, in fact, witnessing a levelling here, men's clothes becoming more visibly feminine and a masculinization of women's attire. Although the patriarchal influences of a recent past are still very marked in the accentuated masculine features of men's clothes, there is likely to be a progressive use of more colour and display. When one recalls the exuberances of baroque times, the distance that can be recovered is realized.

The importance of painting as the emotional yardstick of the day should make the co-operation of the artist and the dress-designer, and indeed of every other form of designer an indispensable one. Materials are, in fact, being designed today by well-known artists, but there is a lingering romantic disdain on the part of the artist to get down to practical applications. There is no reason why painters should not go to painting dresses, as complete works of art, just about the most dynamic visual symbolization that one could devise.

147

The cinema

The ability of the film to generate a sensation of dynamic time and space and so to raise them in fusion to a new symbolic order gives it an advantage over all the other visual arts to break out of the static time and space of the traditional image. What is of special interest to the painter is the ability of the film to bring the artist's work and working in its dynamic aspects to a wider public, perhaps the best and most convincing way of breaking down receptive barriers through creative participation. What Gropius said about architecture applies equally well to painting: 'Nothing promotes an understanding of the environmental planning better than the active participation in it.'

The scanning of a painting by the moving lens of the cine-camera brings out the latent emotional content and helps the eyes to perform their own recreative function; instead of merely looking at a static painting, one begins a dynamic involvement, which can be enormously helped by synergic music and words.

Many interesting experiments have been made in abstract films and thanks to the dynamics of it, some films made in Germany long before the war produced the kind of dynamic valid image which painting has only come upon recently. The application of the moving image to environmental surfaces is perhaps the most powerful means of activating and humanizing them. The movements of people, of traffic, could be televised, appropriately treated and reprojected on even curved surfaces as dynamic abstract appeals, just as the sound of people in the room was used in the Brussels Fair to feed an ever varying 'musique concrète'.

IO

ART AS A CULTURAL BALANCE

SIR HERBERT READ and others have emphasized the role which art should play in education,[78] as the means of ensuring a balanced, harmonious and whole individual. An aspect that needs attention is the reclaim of the specialized individual, increasingly typical of a highly specialized civilization, by the new art.

In the past a cultural discipline and a humanizing view were fostered by a study of the classics, of scripture, of history, of traditional art. There can be no doubt that this provided cultural guide-lines in an age of relative chaos and dismemberment, but the times have gone beyond the ability of such measures to balance the cultural body. The deep reaction against the classical spirit dismisses them. As a result of the failure of the humanities, of past cultural disciplines on the present, the unbalance of our culture is now acute.[79]

The most flagrant product of this unbalance is the scientist and the technical specialist. Experts in their own particular fields, they are frequently moronic in other cultural horizons. A man who happens to be planning a colonization of the planet Venus will find his tastes stopping at Canaletto. This is not only a matter of emotional short-circuit in the individual. It does very much concern the culture as a whole and everyone in it, for scientists are the cultural conditioners: it is most important that they should be whole men.

It has been suggested that science itself could provide the balance, in its native disciplines, in its wider ethical and humanistic applications and obligations. Science has produced its protean figures in men like Darwin, Rutherford, Freud, Einstein, but even a superficial study of such greatness reveals acute discrepancies of character and personality, which can be traced in good measure to an inadequately extended vision of life. However much one stretches the meaning of science, too much is left out to complete the human person. The other alternative is to put into the syllabus of science teaching quite different balancing courses. Since these syllabuses are already crowded, and new demands are constantly being made on teaching time, on learning capacity, this foreign imposition is understandably resisted.

There is a way out, however, namely, by the promotion of an aesthetic view in the very fields of scientific specialization. Every scientific subject is rich in symbolic appeals, capable of serving as genuine examples of the aesthetic function. Although daily handled, these aspects are usually ignored by the specialist. For his entire education and discipline are aimed at an opposite pole of practical interests.

It is a fact that although the aesthetic function is a natural one, the untutored eye is usually less effective as a channel of aesthetic stimulation than the eye which has been made aware of the symbolic power of visible things, of the intrinsically different structure and order of aesthetic appeals. In a true sense, once one has poignantly experienced art, one's eyes and one's mind remain for long conditioned to the instinctive meaning of art, a phenomenon akin to all true conversions of feeling, of the emotional life. And although the underlying function is beyond ordering and rational establishment, it can be favoured by education and by appropriate guidance. To point out to a scientist, looking through his microscope, the essentials of aesthetics in the stimuli and order of his visual experience, is as good as an art lesson; or so it could be. And all the criteria are there. So it is in the fields of the anatomist, of the engineer, of the physicist. If this eye-opening is supported by an ensuing rational treatment of the subject of art and culture, of art and life, of art and psychology, the ability of the eye to see symbolically is progressively developed. Nowhere can one see this more clearly than in music, and it is quite strange that whereas many people will be prepared to accept that this is necessary in the case of music, they will be shy of accepting it in the case of the visual arts. If anything, the practical claims on the eyes are so keen and constant that in order to be able to use the eyes as symbolic conduits, considerably more educational conditioning is required.

Many scientists will admit to what amounts to an aesthetic interest in their subjects and in their specialized activities. It is not only the views which science opens up, the materials and apparatus used that have genuine aesthetic qualities, but the 'language' of science, today symbolic, and the intellectual operations of science have aesthetic aspects as well. An effective theory, the correlation of multiple facts, can have a profound aesthetic impact. Further- more, the intuition which is at the heart of all aesthetic sensitivity has an important role to play in original thinking, in scientific discovery, as many a scientist has discovered. The most original notions usually come like bolts from the blue, often strangely ordered and explicit: the intuitive mind when stimulated can help even the rational order.

To draw notice to the aesthetic aspects of any scientific approach is therefore not only to complete the scientist as a human being, but it can even be of help to him in his work. One can go on to say that the devotion of scientists to their work, at times involving great sacrifice and risk, is fed by an emotional undercurrent which is appealed to by aspects of their life, work, and thought which are essentially aesthetic.

It is to be emphasized that this method of drawing notice to the aesthetic aspects of specialization can go on in the course of ordinary work, study and research; it need not be a foreign subject, a separate course; it can and should be part of the daily scientific life. What is done through wanting is done with interest, and once the scientist's interest in the aesthetic fields of his own subject has been drawn to an experiential level, the natural way is open to lead on to a consistent and related aesthetics, to as wide and demanding a view of art as the scientist should choose to indulge in.

And it is a striking fact that the imageries of the new painting are in close sympathy with many of the views of science. From the perceptual fields of science itself, the most natural roads to the valid arts of our times open up, not by imposition, but by a quite natural progression.

It is a fact, which some of the illustrations in the course of the text should indicate, that many of the imageries of science, with which scientists are in daily contact in the course of their work, are startlingly interesting as aesthetic objects; many are strikingly similar in appeal to quite modern paintings. As already emphasized, there is no borrowing, and no self-respecting artist has looked to science to provide him with cues. The fact is that the new age, climate, and environment have sired new imageries in art which are in close emotional tune with the new imageries of the new world itself, and the hallmark of these new imageries is a radical break with the traditional imagery, in a move to a dynamism and a penetrative symbology already described.

To illustrate the point more specifically, if one were to teach painting to a scientist of the old order, a biologist dealing with organs or a physicist believing in eternal chunks of matter, one would have recourse to traditional technique. To paint a cluster of bones, of organs, of crystals, one would adopt much the same approach and technique as in painting a bowl of apples, for one is still dealing with a concrete world, a realm of fixed and static quantities and shapes. Even in the penetrations of the electron microscope, one finds shadows cast which are identical with the shadows cast by objects in the ordinary world of visual experience. But as soon as one passes to the dynamic happenings of the new physics, of the new chemistry and biology, one is faced with a movement and pulsation, with a perpetual alteration and precariousness, for the portrayal of which the traditional techniques of painting are quite useless. Indeed, as one strives to catch such phenomena by the traditional approaches of observation and exact rendering, one misses their essential quality, and to use various illusional devices to give the impression of movement and pulsation, like the strokes of movement along a racing car, is a subtle form of traditional trickery and cheating. The only way to illustrate such dynamic phenomena is, in fact, to have recourse to the quite new techniques of painting, mostly learnt from the action-painters and abstract expressionists and the practitioners of the other valid imageries. For instance, action-paintings can naturally resemble the exciting photographs of particle tracks and smashed atomic nuclei, the fields of force made evident in paracrystalline structures, the throbbing microstructures within cells, and so on. If a scientist was taught painting, to serve his own fields of observation and experience, it would be with such techniques, and from this, the doors to a truly modern art would be as naturally opened.

Such an approach has various degrees of applicability in almost all specialized fields apart from science. It is directly applicable to the engineer, whose work and normal vision does provide some of the most valid imageries of our present time, and a realization of the aesthetics of which can but help his approaches in themselves. There are also possible applications in industry. Often one finds a particular job liked by one person and found tedious by others: what has happened is that this person has found ways of reconciling himself emotionally to his particular work-situation, and one aspect of this reconciliation is the intuitive finding of emotional satisfaction and gratification in certain aspects of the work done, not only in the objects handled and the movements and attitudes of work, but in the response to the overall stimuli of work, and of the working environment, kinaesthetic, tactile, audio-visual, and human.

It cannot be overemphasized that all material situations are pregnant in symbolic power, and these can be either ignored or encouraged. If the human eye can be blind to physical stimuli, it is far more frequently insensitive to emotional cues, and contrary to physical blindness, this can be corrected by making evident and obvious that which has always been there but ignored. Boredom and apathy are psychological attitudes, and about the most effective way of blocking emotional intercourse with the environment; the challenge to management is obvious.

The value of this approach is that it does provide the basis for a cultural co-operation between art, in its truly valid forms today, and science, technology, and industrialism. In the rise of the Renaissance artists and scientists were drawn together by a common cultural aim. If art could not come together with a science that was disdainful of it, the revisions of view in both art and science make a renewed contact possible and most desirable. A crisis far more acute than the passage of the Middle Ages into the Renaissance is upon us, and the new art, and its direct functional applications in science and in all practical fields of endeavour, becomes the means of restoring an essential co-operation if the modern age is to become humanized and made fit for human survival and fulfilment.

The need for a cultural broadening applies to the artist as well. The separation of art from life and from science in the nineteenth century led to a profound antipathy towards science in most academic art circles: the flagrant materialisms of science and industry were in truth hostile to art, and as a result science and contemporary philosophy were left out of all art education, even in such confusedly mixed territories as architecture, which in spite of its art inheritance has to be practical. Although there are a few attempts at correction, this state of mind persists, and one does find in practice that scientists, for all their limitations, are usually more ready to have a look at art than the other way round. There is also a considerable amount of cultural jealousy involved, for the followers of the arts have not yet fully accepted the fact that it is the scientist who sets the cultural place.

The result of this state of things is that the average product of art schools is narrowminded and, in the fields that matter most today, almost bereft of education and connexion.[80] Such a type is not only unfit to practise or teach art in an age determined almost exclusively by science, but is totally unfit for any form of collaboration with the world-builders of today. If the fault of the break between science and art, art and everyday life, was originally due to a society that had hardened itself against the true functions and meanings of art in human life, the responsibility for providing the right conditions for mending that break today is largely in the hands of artists, and a thorough revision of the type is required. The persisting notion that art is art, a subject apart, and that the best artist is concerned only with art, is a romantic persistence with pernicious consequences to modern life. It is the first correction that has to be made in the education of the artist.

II

THE ETHICS OF ART

THE consequences of the break with nature to both artists and to society are calamitous; it has, as Existentialist writing expresses it, placed man in the face of a void and of an excruciating anguish, for nature has been all to man. More than anyone else, the creative person has felt this isolation, and has sensed the failure of modern life. So he has tended to retreat into himself and to despise society. Yet he remains as always in desperate need of society; art is communication, and the artist who fails to establish it fails and suffers abominably, no matter how great he may believe his art.

The dislike has been mutual, and the picture that the public has built of the artist is often false and mischievous. Invariably a neurotic and difficult to live with, and with a strong libido—there is no art without this—he shows an exasperating disdain of bourgeois convention, of the codes of what most people consider proper behaviour, but he is not an unethical person. If he is utterly selfish where his art is concerned, he is a lover of life, of freedom, for art cannot exist without it, and he has a ferocious hatred of cruelty, of oppression, of pretence, of spiritual corruption, and a deep compassion for his fellow human beings.

It is a fact that the artist cannot cheat himself or the public for any length of time, for he cannot operate successfully by calculation, only by instinct. More often he does things which run him up against the world, against his few friends and admirers, when just a little practical wisdom and stealth would have brought him love and fame. The most potent force in art is the drive towards wholeness, and it accounts for art's sanctifying effect. It cannot be practised in evil, and if art cannot make gods of men, a close acquaintance with it always tends to make men a little more godly than they would have been otherwise. Art has a genetic ethical loading due to its most ancient use of the most humanizing drives of all, the emotionalizing drives towards the noble, the pure and the beautiful within man.

It is not that the cornered artist does not often try to cheat his way out, but it simply does not work when he does. If he persists, he destroys himself. He can but be an instinctive creature, depending on the positive creative aspects of the human psyche, where also all virtues reside. In spite of what the public believes, there simply cannot be a tricked art; art always exists at the instinctive level. This means that if any visual exercise is begun in triviality, it is bound to end in a true aesthetic gesture if persisted in for a sufficient length of time. This aesthetic gratification in any gesture, in any creative approach, has been essential to human evolution, the one drive and reward for the remarkable co-ordination of hand and eye in creative partnership. It is true that even good fakers become involved technically and emotionally in their faking, acquire some at least of the spiritual and emotional powers of those whom they fake, and become possessed.

The artist can but be an artist, an emotionalized, intuitive being, in all he does, in all he thinks. He can see nothing but in the light of his particular stand in art. It is this all-conditioning attitude of the artist that makes him different from others, in whom a more diffuse emotionalism makes possible a variety of attitudes, and even of clashing ones. If an executioner can also be a good churchman, it is quite impossible for the artist to be anything else but an artist in all his actions, attitudes and thoughts. It is this also that makes him disdain so many of the things which others consider so important, loyalties and servitudes, restraints and privileges, which have not and never can have any bearing on any art.

The artist is inherently free, and he must always struggle to remain unbound, uncommitted to everything but his art. It is this that makes every artist an anarchist, a despiser of authority, of the restraints and obligations imposed by authority in any form. These are to him symbolizations of death, of the antihuman.

Over and above an ethical disposition, the artist develops what one might call a professional conscience in the course of his life; he finds his instinctive roots, his instinctive limits, and it is a guiding star that can enable an artist to ride the storms of failure and conspiracy, even of an entire lifetime, and it is the one power that does not decay, but increases in strength with ageing.

Although the artist is fanatical about the success of his art, he is negligent about personal success, about his position in the world of power and prestige; he is often ambitionless there. When an artist begins to seek positions of power, the seat on the committee, the unnecessary lectureship, his creative drive is waning for sure.

Freud was never more wrong than when he implied that the artist practices his art for the love of others and the rewards of adulation. More often, art brings persecution, and in direct proportion to its significance and greatness.

Just as only an age which has faith in itself and its future can produce really great art—all world history proves that point—so the artist to be an artist has to have an inner confidence, an instinctive and unavowed faith in the validity and relevance of his work. But it goes deeper than that. In an inexplicable way, he feels instinctively that his art is something more than a statement on a canvas; there is his lifework, and even beyond that, art has a feeling of transcending time and place, having an enduring time-less quality about it. In an age demanding practical explanations this is very difficult to admit, and most artists tend to dismiss it, but it is there always, a part of their instinctive being. It is almost certainly due to the 'otherness' of art, of its different times and spaces, of its quite other order, an order which may appear a delusion to others with their feet entirely on the material ground, but to the artist it is the one reality. In a true sense, to the artist, and no doubt to every lover of art, art is something that exists in some sort of transcendental sense. An ephemeral view of art is not compatible with great art. Art is for the immortals.

The main test of an artist's integrity comes in the way he releases his works to the dealer and to the public. With a pene-trative image, much time is required for post-creative judgement, and so it is that today many artists create in isolated periods, followed by long intervals of living with their work, of the seventh-day judgement of their creation. The more ruthless the rejection that follows, the greater the artist.

Happiness does not make for a good artist. If the world does not torture him, then he tortures himself. He can never be satisfied with himself.[81] Even disease, some gnawing deformity, can have its creative benefits. At times, creation can be elative, as a sudden uplift of the total emotional life, a sense of imminent participation, but most of the time it is struggle, acute confrontation and fear, fear that the creative fire is not there and will not come again.

In a curious way, the artist stands above himself, and to get to this, he must continually destroy the ties forming about him, and struggle for his freedom, a struggle that goes on in his creative work itself, the refusal of the given, of the easy way out, the continual exposure to creative risk and disaster.[82] It is this incessant fight, within himself and within his art, that makes him an abominable person to live with. Yet, because of this struggle, he needs protection and love, and the strange thing is that he often finds it. Some people, particularly women, appear to sense the divinity of art through all the pettinesses of the artist and are prepared to sacrifice themselves to it. It is a great truth that for the artist the only way to real freedom is in work, in the intensity and absorption of it, and it is in it that he overcomes all bondage and can occasionally rise above himself. Technical challenge and effort are the greatest stimulus. Often when one starts one is apprehensive, the fires are cold; in the manipulation of the materials, they become fanned and roaring, 'l'appetit vient en mangeant'. Unfortunately all stimuli other than work and contact with one's materials are destructive in the end, sex, talk, drugs, change, and travel. A great pity. Sloth is always the symptom of some rodent creative insecurity, some hidden spiritual haemorrhage, and indecision the result of some unsolved neurosis, just as the demented rushing to get things down is a sign of despair and fear not resolved by the struggle of creative effort.

Creation is cyclical, periods of creativity alternating with periods of recharge and stocktaking, even of nihilism. Only the most mediocre creative effort can be continuous. Consistently good work becomes boring, and to go through periods of bad work, even destructive periods, is salutary, just as every technique today incorporates various destructive devices to ensure that the image is kept precarious, on the edge of a continuous precipice. Success must bring failure, or it is destructive to the artist himself, and every success must be followed by a fall, by humiliation and the reminders of the necessity of continued struggle. Unlike others, the artist does not wait for Hubris; he brings it on himself. One can see about one that the artists who have managed to keep up the creative fire in the midst of success are those who have found ways of privation and self-flagellation, physical as well as spiritual.

As much as he must despise success, the artist must resist power, in any form, especially over another person. Nothing corrupts the sensibilities more.

The young are more corruptible by the lures of success, and their need for it more desperate, as the world appears to deny them their due. As one gets older, one comes to accept that ready success is usually deceptive, and in the light of ever faster passing years, even the need for recognition, which is quite another thing, can lose its poignancy. One thing is quite certain; to pursue success is utterly corrupting, for if art is communication, and the artist must do all he can to communicate and to see that his work comes to others, the communication must come from the work and as a result of the work, and never must considerations of its effect go in any way into its making or suggest how it is made. The prospect of success can never be a stimulus to effort in real art, the one division between the man of commerce and the man of sensibility.

Contradiction, and the lack of success, are not synonymous with failure. It is a certain fact that as one begins to accredit success in any human enterprise, so the heads of a gorgonic contradiction arise and appear to flaunt all that one aspires to. This is natural, human, and inescapable. It may frighten the young, and it may exasperate and confuse those who sense a growing failure in their effort or who lack faith, but it does not stop the real artist. Indeed, this kind of a worldly failure is perhaps the keenest test of one's profundity and resilience. An apparent great success can comfort many small men, and mean nothing.

Art is a way of no return; those who are hesitating between the practical world and the emotional, should know beforehand the high price they must pay in choosing the latter. Once one has known the powers of the intuitive order, it is utterly impossible to slip back into the banal and ordinary way of life; everything is branded with a no-return. Finally, one is one's own judge; it does not matter how much others think of one's work if one feels its inadequacies oneself. People can like it or dislike it, that is another matter. And more certainly than anyone else, the artist knows when the creative fountains are running out, an always unpredictable tragedy, that has nothing to do with age, with material hazard, that can come in the midst of splendour; indeed, it is then that it usually comes, seldom after a slow decay; it is, as it were, a more or less sudden departure of the gods, and suicide may well seem the only way out of such a rejection, for the gods never return.

On all fundamental issues the artist is quite alone, and it is this loneliness that sends the lesser-fibred scurrying to the group and into subsidiary activities, into social living, into the orgies of sex and drink. The artist may have to be periodically debauched and needs periodical support and comforting, but never systematically or continually of either; he must be the most assured, self-sufficient person on earth when it comes to the things that matter in his artistic life.

Penetrative appeals are demanding and always inconvenient, and that is why most people avoid them even though there is a clamour in their depths for them. Thus most people are torn between a desire for art and an avoidance of it. Art not only satisfies them, but points out to them their follies, their shallowness and insecurity; so art must be condemned. In this paradox of crisis, at work in society at large, the artist is often crucified, the victory of the external man over the depths. That which I love but cannot possess, that I shall kill. The more significant the art, the more it touches into the instinctive depths, the more ferocious the protest, the stronger the sense of outrage, the more cruel the crucifixion. The artist who explores new paths must expect tragedy in his life; he shall be impaled and quartered, for he is the visible incrimination against the smallness of man, the meanness of the human soul.

Most people feel the humanizing drives at times, and crave for a better world, but to the extent that this is unpractical and would demand untold effort and inconvenience, it is dismissed as the fruits of the passions and the sharp pleasures are indulged in. But the artist must respond in his art to reclaim the world. The work of art is the very first stake of the making of the world after the inner desires of the spirit, which is one good reason why art, however revolutionary and however much readjustment it requires, is always in the end triumphant, and every genuine work of art is a gesture at the reclaim of the fallen world.

The tensions, the loneliness, and the frequent failures of creative enterprise make order essential to every artist, if he is not to break under the strain. Even the most free and apparently abandoned way of working, if it is to have any enduring effectiveness, comes from an ordered, disciplined core of method, of attitude, and if many an artist is apparently disorderly in the common things of life, he is invariably found to be orderly in all that pertains to his art. But the most congenial order is none the less a free order. 'The clear integration of a work of art', wrote Stravinsky, 'and its crystallization demand that the Dionysian elements which stimulate a composer and set in motion the rising sap of his imagination, be adequately controlled before we succumb to this fever and ultimately be subordinated to discipline'. The artist tends to be a Dionysian person, and he is periodically wantonly so, but his real creative achievements always coincide when he can surmount this potential threat to disruption, chaos and annihilation. The artist who becomes overrun by his Dionysian inclinations is done for.

12

ART AND RELIGION

Religion can be defined as a belief in the transcendental significance of human emotionalism; if the aspirations, yearnings, and desires for beauty and peace, for harmony and purity, for grace and goodness, for selflessness and a sense of duty and love for others, can all be traced to the primordial emotionalization of sex, then it is these same aspirations and yearnings that can be used in the spiritualization of the human being, the raising of the entire emotional level into a quite new world of experience.[83]

But as soon as such a statement is made, the impossibility of a proper definition of what we really mean by religion is realized, for the emotionalized core on which it depends is itself indefinable and quite irreconcilable with reason and good logic. So in all religious matters there is always one aspect clamouring for definition and explanation, for making religion known, and there is another and its essential part which is beyond all definition: in a very true sense, religion can only be experienced to be known, like art and all essentially emotional matters.

This inexplicability of the essential core of religion is a fact that must be admitted at the start, for the urge to know, to define, is a human one and is always interfering. Here the artist has an advantage, for he is the type of person who does not clamour for such precision. Emotional truth for him is truth; there is none other. And it is this same contact and reliance on the emotional order which makes every artist in some sense religious, for it is a part of the emotional function to work itself out in transcendental ways, of which art itself is the clearest example. Religion is only one other aspect of this same tendency, and so it is that art comes to fortify the religious view, for it is identical in origin and process. Accordingly, art, and especially the penetrative kind of art we are dealing with, can have something to say on religion.

It is frequently assumed that religious feeling must be related to some organized faith, to some theology. But this need not be so at all. This attachment and dependence is only necessary at one stage in the evolution of religious feeling, in much the same way that art in its evolution has depended at one stage on nature. One can go farther and say that the natural tendency of this evolution is for religion, like art, to evolve out of its supports and gain an ever greater degree of freedom. The progressive freeing of religious feeling from such supports, in the form of doctrines, established religions and churches, is a fact of our times, and it is quite a wrong viewing of the case to assume that what is widely happening today means a loss of religious feeling. People are as religious as ever, basically. The fact that human beings continue to behave to all appearances ethically and religiously, whether they have avowed beliefs or not, proves that the religious function, intuitive and mostly unrealized, is a force in itself and quite separable from all supports. There are many religious features in some of the most avowed anti-religious doctrines of today,[84] in their ability to bring out sacrifice, a sense of duty, and devotion to cause and effort, to transcendental goals.

If it is likely that human beings are passing over into a stage when religious feeling can, in fact, become severed from all its previous supports, from theology, it means that these supports should be dispensed with here and now and religion approached from now on as an entirely personal adventure. This need not amount to a denial of the theological interest,[85] but it does mean that it is no longer essential to religious acknowledgement. Nor does this mean that religion is to become an egocentric occupation. In every aspect of it, it serves the individual as a creature in human society and in human fellowship. But it does mean that organized, formulated, explicit approaches are from now on unnecessary and misleading, for any such formulation must, by the nature of the case, in some way constrain and interfere with the free emotionalism of religion. The analogy with a naturalistic, figurative art is pertinent.

In what follows therefore no attempt is made to offer a religious doctrine, but rather to suggest the many similarities and analogies of art in its valid forms today with a kindred religious feeling which in some form or other is probably essential as ever to the complete human being.

Like art, religion is not compatible with reason and rational analysis. It has been one of the fallacious claims of an Age of Reason that reason is the highest human virtue, a belief that has led to some of the most hideously unreasonable beliefs and actions. Mankind will be better off when the limitations and deceptions of reason have been unmasked. A religion of rationalism is an absurdity.[86]

But it is very necessary to emphasize that to put reason in its place does not mean opening the doors to irrationalism, to chaos, and superstition. The struggles of science against the established religions are close enough to make this point necessary, for no matter how curtailed reason may have to be, it is impossible to admit the irrational, as a denial of all order, as a denial of the possibility of all human knowing. Irrationalism is the angered and morbid reaction of the soul choked by reason. An irrational Universe would be an insane Universe. Art shows clearly the existence of quite different possibilities of order, and religion can depend on a view of the Universe which remains orderly and yet is not restricted to the reasonable or material. The claims of the material order remain as valid as ever, but the Universe becomes extended to contain other orders as well, knowable by the oldest of human faculties, emotional symbolization.

Materially, the time of the clock, regular and unalterable, seems final and all-conditioning. Yet other kinds of time can be entertained, even by science,[87] and art is the proof of quite a different order of experiential time, as it is of space.[88] Human beings live continually, in their emotionalized inner core, with a quite other and different order, with a quite different meaning of time and space, the promise in all things, if we but look at them in the right way, of man's potential freedom from the bondage of time and space. Dynamically, which is the view of both art and science today, time and space lose their separateness and merge into some tremulous condition which is outside the limitations of ordinary visible material space and its time. The mind has it within its own emotionalized functions, and to some extent in all thought, to sense its essential unboundedness.

A Universe of infinite spaces and times is more rational than a finite one, with only one time and space of material happenings. Man's possible participation in this universal system, promised in his mind itself and evident in his art and experienceable in his religious feelings, is none the less quite unspecifiable and undefinable. The sensing of it intuitively is its entire experience. To talk of the 'survival of death', of 'immortality', is evidence of intellectual limitation, the eternal canker of reason's demands for artificial definition and precision. Humility as much as faith is the required virtue, and it is surely a most remarkable and sufficient thing that man can have some awareness of time's mystery, of the possibility that the ordinary notion of the passage of time by the clock is not reliable and unique, and that other times may run concomitant with it.

Although an Age of Reason has made certainty appear as the most desirable thing, it is rather doubt that is natural to the human condition. Any definite statement is the invitation to a denial of it, and the proper attitude to the mystery of life is not a belief that human understanding can come to solve it entirely, but rather to accept the impossibility of a final knowing. It is precise knowing that is perforce limited; the knowing of the heart and of the emotions have no limits. In the auroral light of dawn, one feels that one knows all things.

And there can be no progress and passage from one kind of knowing to the other. With the knowing of the worldly realm, one can learn, but in all that is emotional, there must be a jump into quite another order, as the experience of art shows so well.

It is worldly knowing that is alloyed with animal doubt, the doubt of the material animal that fears that it is no more than animal. Yet this doubt is in itself useful. For those who contend that a dogmatic and explicit faith is necessary for humanizing behaviour, it is well to point out that in the ages of so-called faith, human beings were never more heartless and ruthless to one another. With the rise of the doubt fed by materialism, at least a majority of persons have become socially aware. From the position of anguishing doubt, man comes to sense the need to transcend his doomed and caged physiological status and the absolute necessity of his spiritualization. It is in this sense that the anguish and isolation of Existentialism can become the source of hope. Although the collapse of the traditional faiths has been necessarily succeeded by Existentialism, this may be no more than a temporary phase in some sort of recovery of confidence in being and existing, encouraged by a revised viewing of man's place in the Universe, a Universe not hostile to life as materialism saw it, but on the contrary congenial to it, a Universe potent in mystery and wonder.

In art today man is already beyond nature, indeed beyond himself. The pilgrimage goes on, in a universal creative enterprise in which man can find an honourable place.

Only space-fiction writers have so far explored the implications of a cosmic universality of man. The kinds of human-like creatures which different planetary natures could produce are no doubt innumerable. On our own planet, the existing variations within one interbreeding species are striking enough, and the experiments of the past in man-making have produced strange and terrifying simulacra of manhood. But if one had enough facts, it would be possible to come to a cataloguing of this diversity. It is more than likely that the human earth-type could be bettered; somewhere, superior examples of what we might have been may well have been produced. We are visibily deviant creatures, in our habits and thoughts, in our food, in our sex, in our drives and desires. The conditions of human creation on this planet have, in fact, been sub-optimal, and so it is that we are all aware of a certain possibility of greater perfection, of purer love, of undefiling food, of a natural grace and peacefulness, which we fail most usually to attain in a world of existential compromises, resorting to a common behaviour which on some sort of cosmic scale must amount to subhuman behaviour. But the fact that we can sense the type to which we might have belonged is not only the source of our dilemma, that must for ever prevent us from enjoying simply and without reproach an animal and subhuman existence; it can also be a stimulus to correction through human effort. Now that man is fast gaining a final control over nature and entirely supplanting her, the primordial source and responsibility for his imperfections can be surmounted—provided only that man can create in his synthetic environment a state superior to nature.

What we need to know and to accept is the type of our potential selves, the essence that lies beyond the existential. It is there clearly enough; with greed aside, one can see quite clearly the sex of the Fall, and the love which could be truly human, as much as we can see the food of the Fall, our usual fare and consumption, to the kind of food compatible with man's purity and spiritual ascension. Whether or not such a type has ever been attained on earth does not matter; sensing it, we could aspire to it. In the fields of feeling the deviations are legion and chronic. There is a music and an art of Fallen Man, just as there is an Arcadian music, a painting of heaven and a painting of hell. But it is also true that art, to be art at all, always retains a breath of the wholeness and purity which belongs to the Man of Paradise. In art, man can always find exercise to the promise of an emotionalized humanism, usually denied him on this planet in other respects, yet which he can now set about winning through his own efforts, environmental as much as a revolution in feeling and orientation.

For man, the symbolic animal, the symbolic view of all things is the only view. Material reality for him can but end in an illusion.[89] It is not the ability of the child, of the primitive, and of the artist to see everything symbolically that is strange, but rather the rationalist's and the materialist's attempt to limit experience to the demands of reason and materialism.

The only possibility of a final illusion is that the Universe is not at heart symbolic, and that the symbolic perceptions of man are, like all else, a delusion. Yet, as man has penetrated with his observation and knowledge, even in his materially limited sciences, he has found that a basic reality, whatever that be, is only amenable to symbolic approaches. But of far greater assurance, the symbolic experiences of art, and of religion, can bring a degree of heightened conviction and reality-feeling that finally dispels all possibility of this quandary. Like art, true individual religious experience, as opposed to the charades of it in organized and habitual religion, seems to confirm the existence of a supersymbolic realm, to which the human mind has access, which provides an utterly undeniable perception once experienced. It is this that feeds faith, the ability to see through reason and doubt, and to have an implicit reliance on the entire transcendental order of things. Most artists have this instinctively and art in its great moments can enforce it in a way very similar to religious experience.

Creation, in art as in the Universe at large, is not the kind of precise, deterministic affair that the human mind requires. On the contrary, it is opportunistic, 'open', potentially infinitely variable. This shocks the uniqueness demanded by an ethics of reason as to the value of man, of life, yet it can also be seen as the most generous and wide-reaching creative mechanism. A straight creation would be bound to run to an end; an opportunistic creation is inexhaustible.

A mechanistic view of creation also expects perfection and precision. Creation in art and life simply do not work that way, but on the contrary remain free and open. In the course of this, there is bound to be quandary and struggle, waste and elimination, but that is the way of things, tragic on the short count, but refreshing on the long run.

The spiritual emergence comes with the emergence of man from the animal, and is accompanied by tragic and fierce struggle. All religions emphasize this. There is always a scale of creative achievement, stretching from the banal to the highest spiritual reaches. As the heights are reached, so all that has gone before becomes vestigial. Man is a moving museum of vestiges, not only physical, but emotional and spiritual as well. Effort is always involved in the rise to the emerging higher levels, and once reached, although fall is possible and even probable, there is always a price, a measure of insatiation, and a devise for renewed effort, the necessary inset goad of an evolving Universe.

An evolving, self-regulating Universe has inbuilt corrections to wayward and irregular accidents or decisions. These are evident in the living animal, in the brain and mind; they must in some way apply on a planetary level as well; planets, like species of animals, fail to survive, and there may well be planetary diseases of elimination just as among living things.

Deeply inbuilt into the human psyche there appears such a controlling device in the form of conscience. Although a materialistic age has tended to look upon conscience and guilt as artificial and unnecessary things, they serve a function, demanding readjustment, usually following some offence against deep human roots, in bestiality, in greed and in an animal sexuality, for which the human being has not been conditioned.

Guilt is accompanied by grace. The disquiet in man's mind is the price of failing to attain the promise of the spiritual in him and the creep down to levels of behaviour which are intended to be vestigial. In this state of torment, relief can be provided only on one condition: that a renewed attempt is made at readjustment and reintegration. It is a fact of common experience that wrong thought or action by any code bring about guilt, and guilt as naturally demands grace as a temporary respite to make a renewed effort possible. And it is a fact known to every psychiatrist that unless such grace is forthcoming, then guilt is apt to destroy, one good way of eliminating the spiritually unfit.

Great art can atone, redeem. It brings wholeness to the

emotional life, it purifies, it ennobles and bleeds away disturbing
tensions and the corrosive fluids of remorse and guilt. It is
sanctifying.

One of the universal services of religion is to promote a feeling
of participation in a process greater than the individual. Although
this cannot be consciously ordered, it can be prepared for in a
variety of ways, in various rites and ceremonies, in dance, in
listening to music and contemplating works of art, even by the
use of drugs. Illumination comes as a kind of sudden ecstasy.
Once it has been profoundly experienced, life can never be the
same again, nothing without some spiritual correspondence.
There is something analogous to this in art, and the use of
pyote, the 'sacred mushroom', has apparently the same
affect.

This synergy of art and religion in bringing about a climax to
religious experience is best pursued in special places and sanc-
tuaries, the ancient function of the temple. Today, this would have
to be in completely universal forms and without any doctrinal
restrictions, providing refreshment, peace, and human reassurance
to all, and combining the artist, the psychiatrist, the doctor in a
reunited service to the human being in his desire not only for
solace but for wholeness of being.

If drives and energies are to be found for other purposes, then
the libido must be canalized and diverted. So it is that neither
society, nor religion, nor art for that matter, can thrive without
some sort of control over sexual opportunism, and they all
demand some sort of transcendentalizing of the sexual impulse,
the raising of the levels of feeling into love, social service, religious
experience. Society has always insisted on some sort of control
over sex, and a world-wide mysticism resorts to sexual descriptions. Love, evident in all mysticism, finds its strength in the most
basic of all human fountains, the one force that can take man
beyond himself.

The transfiguration of sex in both art and religion forces a
dualism, at times tormenting, for on the one hand there is the
simple, immediate appeal of physical sexuality open to all animals
and still insown in the vestigial mind of man, best enjoyed by the
removal of all restraints, and on the other 'the higher satisfactions'
which are incompatible with such simplicity. So it is that the
raising of man beyond the animal level has been accompanied by

a desperate struggle between the prehuman and the humanizing, a struggle essential to religion.

The tendency for the 'male' and 'female' elements to become fused emotionally in the work of art has been mentioned, and this fusion does, in fact, reflect a higher state of achievement over the more primitive sexual demarcations. All love strives towards such an androgyny, towards less personalized, less sexually marked and more universal forms. But this does not proceed without much struggle and opposition. The tragedies of history are there to show it.

And the reality of the 'fall', as some catastrophic dehumanizing event in the early days of man on earth, probably in the form of the ice ages, must be taken into account. Ours is a fallen world, in which the process of humanization goes on under great difficulties, and often crippling handicaps. So that a progressive humanization, depending on the spread of love which is part of the natural religious drive, can only come with much effort and struggle. Yet this is the one opening to a universal brotherhood of man, and the restitution of the reality of religious feeling is perhaps an essential requirement for this to be taken on again where the great theological religions left it in their decline. Some day, this primordial propensity to love may well have to be stretched to an interplanetary scale, as we discover other beings on other planets, in other galaxies.

The fundamental dualism between the animal antecedents, the prehuman and the humanizing, the old and the 'new man', becomes expressed in various concrete forms as a struggle between darkness and light, between angels and devils. As society becomes more complex, so the frustrations increase, and so the primitive aspects of the mind become aroused, and the devils increase their clamour and their sway (p. 6). The evidence of this increase can be found in both art and religion. It is probably true that under benign conditions there is barely need for religion. Religion, like art, is a means of emotional adaptation, and evolves with increasing cultural complexity. The highest religions, like the most evolved forms of art, occur in the most complex societies, and it is significant that if art in the most complex of all civilizations has had to go abstract, so is religion in its own ways getting rid of its bondages and becoming the religion of pure experience.

An emotional regard for purity, for wholeness and harmony, is part of man's humanizing reaction to nature (p. 55). In art, one can get a similar emotion from its integration and wholeness, from the transmutation of things that goes on in all art. It is also possible for this sense of purity, deeply ingrained in the psyche and part of it, to be made aware of itself by contemplation of the impure, and in that sense it is not at all puritanical, the cry for love in the charnel house, for purity in the brothel.

An appreciation of purity is essential for all religious experience, although it can take strange forms, as in the demand for a 'virgin birth' common to some of the great religions. Human beings have an innate realization that sex, in a fallen world, is itself unwhole and corrupting. It becomes necessary to cleanse the mystery of birth by removing sex from it.

In art, certain imageries more than others have a power of inducing a sense of purity, of sanctity in the 'meta' and 'soft edge' painting, for instance. The puritanical extreme, however, as one finds it in the geometric image, ends in the denial of all sex, of all somatic feeling and ends in an emotional death.

Another claim of all the great religions, which cannot be understood rationally, is the paradox of person and something which is more than person in everyone. Art offers an analogy in the communal, transpersonal influences (see p. 100). Since the emotional half of man is quite different from the external order, the apparent fusion of externality and internality that one finds in the common moments of life is a convenient illusion; the fundamental difference between an 'inner' and an 'outer' aspect of man remains. The inner, so evident in the symbolizations of it in art, is free, not bound by the restrictions of space and time, and so while being in one paradoxical sense personal, it can also be transpersonal. The more penetrative one's approach to personality becomes, so the more paradoxically trans-personalized it becomes. It would be quite profitless to attempt to define this further in the words of common reason, but it does appear to be a fact of experience. Religious emotion belongs specifically to the extensions of the human being into such trans-personalized aspects, and it is from here that there comes the feeling of participation in something greater, even infinite.

Man has been designed to be humane, and one of the essentials of being human is to feel compassion for one's fellow beings. All animals no doubt feel much the same sort of thing for their young.

A radiative human compassion, unless it becomes bounded by hate and by other defeats of humanization, is the most fundamental human attitude, and one does find it to be so among the most truly primitive people. It is lost with the complicating rise of culture and civilization, and it is only eventually restored after an agonizing circle by the emergence of the great religions and of humanism. A religious humanism can be looked upon as the making explicit and effective of a tendency long smothered by inhumanism, the development of a necessity for human beings to be human, always encouraged by the great religions, but now pursuable in itself. Humanism appears as the natural successor of the great world religions. To think that man can survive without some sort of religion is folly. Today, only some form of humanism is likely to take on and develop the genetic religious sense.

Compassion is a force that can become radiative to all things, to all living things, even to matter. Humanism should be able to embrace the entire Universe.

One of the oldest functions of religion has been to provide totems and effigies with the co-operation of artists to act as socially binding, community-consolidating emotional nuclei. As Jung emphasized, this function runs deep. Today, both art and religion have moved on to less embodied and more free processes, less tied to primitive, possessive, and archetypal passions, and so capable of better service to a universal humanity, a world-wide communion of human beings.

Just as much as freedom is essential to art, so every artist is intuitively sensitive to the sacredness of life; it is an inseparable coupling of the keeness and ability to create. Of course, an artist can exist on a plurality of compromised planes, like anyone else, but if the average person can get away with it, an existence which would disregard life, aid in its misery and pain, could but interfere and blunt the creative faculties.

Yet, as is everyone, the artist can but be aware of the misery, frailty, and cheapness of life. How can such a thing be sacred? Here indeed is the crucial dilemma of any religious view. Every existence begins at a point in time, and if the human creature in any sense is able to transcend time—the only possible source of his sacredness in a material realm which flouts all his inner dignities— then it can but be in one of two ways: that he participates in a Universe which naturally contains such an extension in all things, heightened in the human creature, or else that human conception is an extraordinary event, a miraculous occurrence in which the human being acquires some sort of privilege not granted to the rest of creation.

Christianity reacted against a pantheistic view of a creation which was entirely sacred: a more materialistic and reasonable view of life would obviously clash at every point with such a view. So man became seen in Christianty as a creature especially divine, the exclusive aristocrat of all creation. At some stage in the creation of every human being there had to be an act of divine intervention, and one can see the importance the Roman Catholic attaches to conception and the iniquity of any interference with it. But this dangerous dichotomy becomes ridiculed in the compromises of Protestantism, while the Catholic can only maintain it by a stand which runs against all modern realizations and against eugenics, a fast-growing imperative. The only consistent way out of this anomaly is a view of the innate native sacredness of all things, and the essentially miraculous nature of all being, an admission in which man can be legitimately seen as the height of incarnation and the paragon of embodiment.

The artist knows well a similar kind of dilemma, and comes to a comparable resolution of it, for art begins always and necessarily at a point in time, with no pre-existence. If it is confusing to conceive of a pre-existence outside the work of art in the artist's mind—this idea, we have seen, no longer applies to the new art—in being 'born' in space and time, in matter, the work of art also acquires a symbolic 'life' that transcends it. Art breathes the pivotal drama of man, the paradox of material and transcendental existence.

All religions have two very opposite attitudes, towards 'works' and action, and towards meditation; one cannot fail to see the similarity in the 'energetic' and the 'quietist' imageries in painting today.

The religious equivalent of the energetic in art is 'spiritual quickening', the giving of symbolic 'life', the emergence of the new humanizing spirituality, of 'life' in a sense not limited to space and time, the promise of 'life' as opposed to 'death', which in the terms of the spirit is the over and done with, the vestigial within man, which man must surmount and discard in order to reach his full spiritual stature. It is no coincidence that the symbols of life all over the world are closely tied to symbols of death; in dying to his ancestral and existential self, man is born as an emotionalized, spiritual being.

The object of all meditation is to approach some sort of emotional 'centre' within the psyche which seems to have an enormous capacity to unite, fuse, and boost emotionalized awareness (p. 9). This 'centre' is quite unapproachable consciously; one simply cannot order one's way into it. It is about the most remote yet powerful nether land of the human psyche. At times one can get a glimpse of it in the radiative wholeness and penetration of art, in certain Zen practices. In the past, traditional meditative practices and prayer were often effective also, but today they fail. The reason is that the centre must be alive, and fed by live, deeply sensed feelings. As long as human beings believed in a 'living God', it served as an effective centring device. Prayer also requires a removal from life which is not possible today. Modern man is 'engaged' in all his aspects. So it is that the quietism of the 'cool' imageries in painting suggests a way out, in 'active contemplation'.

The religious function comes into its own in the clash of man and nature. When the break is not too severe, religion, like art, is 'naturalistic'. When the break is more complete, religion becomes more entirely man-centred and even anti-nature, as one finds in the Christianity of the Existentialists like Kierkegaard. Then 'natural man' becomes corrupt, fallen, and salvation is seen as the break with the 'old Adam', with man's naturalistic past. As in art, this puts man in a heart-searching dilemma, amounting to a denial of his most ancient roots. It is a fact that the death of nature in the industrial environment has also synchronized with the death of the old religions in man's heart, and it has become necessary for any truly contemporary religious view to see the break with nature, not as an irremediable tragedy, but rather as the means of further evolution.

It is not only that industrialism is antinature in method and spirit, but the fact that nature has always been suboptimal for the function of a fuller humanization; at some time or other, man would have been bound to go beyond nature, in order to become fully human. The 'goodness' of nature is a romantic fallacy. Most of man's evils can be traced to a dehumanizing nature. The beauty of nature conceals the venomousness of the lurking snake, and if it is true that by his efforts man has at times and then only rarely managed to bend nature more to his own wishes and requirements, nature on this planet as a whole, while promoting the creation of man, has not been appropriate to his full and unblemished manhood. Naturalistic cultures have in the longer run done more harm than good in that they have maintained the deceit and have allowed human beings to believe that nature was on the side of man. Those who subscribe to 'back to nature' movements are doing a great human disservice. At the present crisis in human survival, anti-nature movements would be more appropriate, helping to wean mankind finally from a nurture that has been hurtful and malformative. Only then will it be possible to treat the synthetic environment seriously, to strive to make it wholly satisfying and to respect those limits, set by nature, it is true, which man cannot trespass without tragedy of mind and body.

In one form or another desire is the source of all human effort. A lesson that one can learn from the analogy of sex and art, already referred to repeatedly, is the fact that desire is only creatively encouraging when it is still in the form of desire. There is, as it were, an insown assurance that any desire that becomes satisfied produces insatiety in its wake—the accumulation of wealth invariably brings its dissatisfactions, if it only amounts to a blunting of the simpler pleasures of life, and the more physical pleasures of sex are notoriously followed by the 'triste post coitus'.

The pursuit of art, however, appears to contradict this general rule, and so does the religious experience; there, one finds enhanced satisfaction free of conditions, of insatiation. The reason for this may be simple: Evolution can only proceed by internal and external goads which tend to make animals do the things essential for their survival and so for their continued development. As one stage follows another, so it is the new stage that must be made attractive, and the previous stage made somehow unattractive. So as sex became emotionalized, a purely physical sex, although still very enjoyable, acquired certain unsatisfactory ingredients, which indeed only disappear if union is thoroughly emotionalized. And so it is within the mind; as the spirit emerges in the emotionalized inner world of man, so other levels of emotional existence become somewhat less attractive. How true this is in the field of art; when we have come to taste 'high art', anything else invariably lacks enjoyment.

Every artist knows that a rapid emptying of creative desire is the most certain way of bleeding it white; desire must be maintained, and the teachings and techniques of art, which often seem unnecessarily laborious to an outside person, are just such ways of maintaining desire. No artist can ever attain a complete satisfaction in what he does, for his entire approach and method is not that of the voluptuary: he insists on maintaining the potential of desire. Higher levels of desire are, in fact, satisfying, just because they can be maintained and enhanced, without the primitive call to cash.

If the significance of evolution is not so much in the achievement of new things as in the attainment of new levels of being, levels are not entirely without connexion, although entirely different. Complex molecules at the borderlands of livingness, if one imagines them as conscious, might well be able to have some sense of what life is about, although it would be entirely different from their ordinary condition. So 'correspondence', as Rimbaud, Swedenborg, and de Chazal[90] have stated in their different ways, can enable man to sense the higher significance of things, above his present attainments and yet through them. For all things can be seen by the mind, in its unceasing quest for higher levels of spiritual being, to possess supersymbolic powers, powers of indescribable revelation, from the banal to the utterly inexpressible.

It is easy enough to experience at lower levels, but in order to experience the function of correspondence, one must not only be free from the vestigial, but from the existential as well, from all lower and existing levels. Once completely free from nature, man may even use nature for transcendental purposes, should he so choose to do, but when he has superseded nature in life and in actuality, it is much more likely that his emergent spiritual needs will be met by things which nature cannot provide, by opportunities for correspondence and for transcendance nowhere to be found but in an emerging aesthetic level itself. The highest and most spiritually connected art can but be abstract, and an abstract order which has no back references to a lower state of natural dependence, but on the contrary emphasizes man's transcendance of that dependence.

In this groping for symbolic ascension through all things visible and invisible, and through things created entirely by man for his innermost and highest needs, one can sense a difference in the intensity of religious feeling and experience, a lower and more existential kind, which is essentially adaptative, giving to man a present comfort and wholeness, and a far more remote and yet active kind that drives man from any stability and present security of spirit into the transcendental, the unrealized, and the all-demanding world of transfiguration, of correspondence and of transcendence, the higher borderlands of spiritual evolution not yet attained and consolidated. It must also follow that this last kind can but be a rare and paroxysmal experience.

Death has always been and always will be an utterly intolerable event to human beings. As Mircea Eliade points out, even more than love, death constantly preoccupies all primitive peoples, and mythical activities have but one overriding aim—to confront death and to find a way out of its intolerable dilemma.

There is only one other alternative: to avoid confrontation with death, and it is this that we have adopted with materialism. By various ruses, by so-called simply living, one assumes that one has managed to dismiss death, and this can be practised under conditions where death abounds, in times of war and cataclysm. But this apparent dulling to the fact and implications of death is only very superficially successful. In fact, if modern man thinks that he can consciously ignore death, his unconscious is harassed and continually preoccupied with it, as the persistent interest in crime, in violent tragedy and morbidity testify. It is better to entertain it consciously, for then man is brought to a state of crisis that nothing further can surpass. As an animal without religious feeling, this confrontation can but be terrifying, utterly negating and humiliating. Yet, even as such, he displays some evidence of an instinctive defiance and transcendence of the fact of physical death, in his actions, in his frequent scorn of it in courage and self-annihilation, that indicates that in his emotional depths man does possess a natural mechanism to meet this crisis, beyond all avowed religion, and quite instinctively. The value of a conscious confrontation is that it raises this mechanism to more explicit, organized, and effective levels. In fact, most people, sooner or later, are brought face to face with death in the act of dying, apart from the mercy of accidental and sudden death, and the risk is that such an unrehearsed terminal confrontation not only produces an extreme anguish and crisis of utter hopelessness, but the possible value of it to living is lost. And the value of it is that as man faces death by his own choice, in thought and even in reality, so he becomes aware of the total dismay of an essentially physical, material existence. From this dismay, and from out of its horror and terror, springs an instinctive and powerful obligation for transcendence. This need not, indeed cannot, be conscious, explained, made explicit; it can but be emotional, a matter of deep feeling. But that is sufficient. How, why, and to what end, do not matter at all. As a fact, man, as an emotionalized creature, can, in terms of an emotionalism which in the midst of life does transcend space and time, meet death and sense it instinctively as a thing apart from him, different, as matter is different, and it is here that the Existentialists, like the Medieval mind, senses in death a positive and not a negative entity. A purely physical consideration of death completely annihilates man as an emotional, feeling creature, and his only possible reaction is one of paramount rebellion and defiance. From this anarchy against the material power over him, man does obtain from his depths a fantastic surge of power, a source of power in life and through death which is as old as man. And who can dare say that he is wrong in deriving it, that the emotional assurance he obtains from the springs of his emotional being are not in some quite inexplicable way a true defiance of death, of time and matter?

As a painter essentially concerned with the creation of intensely vital imageries, the writer has found as a matter of experience that the most intense expressions of vitality frequently come from an acute and most poignant awareness of death, of its assault against the dignity and establishment of life. As a constant companion, accepted and entertained, it becomes the most powerful proclaimer of the rights of life. Death is such a power that it can become all-claiming; there are many examples in the history of art and religion of this risk of necrophily, but it is possibly true that without an acceptance of the dialectic of life and death, there can be no full realization of the meaning of life for man.

The fact and horror of pain and suffering has been a perennial sore to any religious optimism, and the most usual way out is to find some virtue in it. One rightly senses that this is a smug affront, that somewhere in the argument there is deceit. Aesthetics has a point to make in this issue. The appreciation of art, as of music, is quite incompatible with pain. Now, if art is a natural, genetical activity, and the appreciation of beauty and harmony are natural faculties, then it would appear to follow that any agency that negates them is unnatural. It is a fact that hideous things, evilsmelling things, just as much as nasty-tasting foods, are pathologizing. Ugliness, as opposed to beauty, is antihuman. And so is pain. In all his right instincts, man rejects and abominates pain, and it is his task to fight it at every turn, to do all in his power to overcome it. Pain is in truth the price one pays for living in a fallen world, and to the extent that man struggles to establish the earthly paradise, so he combats pain as the greatest enemy. But man does live in a fallen world, where pain abounds, and therein pain can acquire a certain existential value in that it is not only the dialectic of some beatific condition without pain and so makes one aware of one's existential distress and wanting, but it can, like the torment of death, act as a shock to one's self-awareness and so acquire existentially constructive and even enjoyable properties. In a comparable way, ugliness can acquire positive aesthetic appeal and merit, and can be heartily enjoyed, even more than a beauty grown anodyne and largely meaningless to existentially gripped human beings. To others, who are not in such a grip of an anguished and harassed existence, this may well appear as an affront. The danger of masochism, as in an art that glories in the sordid and ugly, lies just here, for in failing to find the purer desires of his innermost heart, the human being is only too apt to transfigure and transmute the values of his fallen world into positive appeals. But this transfiguration remains secondary, and, in a very fundamental sense, non-human; if accredited with positive power, it becomes antihuman. So if one can find, at least for some persons and in certain situations, a secondary value in pain, none the less it remains the supreme evil and must be combated and overcome in every instance.

Every artist has his peak, and many forms of physical decline bring his art to an end. There are also particular virtues in the expressions of youth, as of maturity. But the remarkable thing is that some artists manage to continue to develop in defiance of physiological decay, even of severe disease. Verdi composed his most magnificent opera in his eighties, and today a great composer like Stravinsky continues to develop with breathtaking speed. If the bulk of Beethoven is felt today to be out of tune with modern feeling, his last quartets, composed when he was sick and dying, have remarkable insights into modernity and a profundity quite outside his previous periods. So it has been with painters like Rembrandt, Cézanne, Monet.

If one looks at this strange phenomenon a little more closely, one sees that it is the more superficial expressions that fade with ageing. A composer of vaudeville, a painter of the passing scene, will steadily lose his edge as his hormones decline and his eyes dull. But if it is the deeper spirit that is involved, then there is the possibility of continued growth in defiance of physical decay. Indeed, physiological limitations may well enhance the process at an earlier age: it is a fact that some of the greatest artists have suffered from poor vision; the inner light of the eye was to them more important than the outer. Where does this defiance end? Is man entirely a creature of time and material space, or does he over-ride them in some way inexplicable to reason? At least there would appear to be a hint of it. Possibly that strange dramatic sense, so acute in the European (p. 70), comes from an intuitive realization of this possibility combined with a more reasonable feeling that man is not up to the mark, that the taste is nothing but a teasing, and yet man must live on . . . 'le vent souffle, il faut tenter de vivre' . . . Yet the challenge is there, man makes himself, and it is up to him and that which he can even dimly perceive is surely potentially his.

Art has rediscovered the meaning and value of paradox. Not as a chronic inability to make clear, to reduce to final causes, but as something at the very heart of things, the oscillation and trembling of all things that makes for the new and the endlessly striving, the clash of opposites that makes for the completely new synthesis. In this state of things, an attempt to be precise is folly. It is a feeling of the dynamism of things that matters.

And just as the new art teaches that the most fundamental, really human experience is not one of certainty but of paradox, of ambiguity, of elusiveness, of mystery that makes reason appear such a limited instrument, so the religious view has itself moved on from the static and precise to the dynamic. Religion becomes not a standing back, a contemplation, an act of meditation, but on the contrary an act of committing oneself dynamically, of living, of being, and of realizing one's germinal potentialities, and above all, of implicitly accepting the reality, the 'isness' of things.

An awareness that comes from art and religious experience makes one see everything, every problem, every desire and encounter in something of a different light; it is no longer just an event, a thing, an object, a person; it has extensions, a continuity of meanings, and one can soon sense a grading in this; things, and objects, and people that have more extensive significance. Many people drift through life in a virtual conditioned reflex, eating, sleeping, fornicating, and in the reflex pursuit of those many claims and clatters of daily living. It is not that these should be denied, but once one has had a religious view of things, it can no longer be only this; there is the indefinable more, and a person who has come to this experience has an aura of awareness about him which does make him different.

These are the aware and the unaware, and it goes out into even the smallest act, whether one smokes, what one thinks of things, of everything. If for no other reason, religion is important in providing this sense of awareness; art provides a very close analogy in 'meaning', the instinctive appreciation of aesthetic value.

Once one has come upon the 'meaning' of a work of art, of a particular idiom, a completely new boundless world of feeling is opened up, which alters everything, oneself, one's environment.

Religious emotion is natural, and in all probability the human being cannot be quite whole and complete without it. Art, so close to it in mechanism and in appeals, can no doubt go some good way in helping to provide its failure. But this closeness of function has greater social meaning. It is possibly true that if only a restless, anxious age produces much art, great art can only come in periods of restoring harmony.

The intensity of the crisis of modern man is to all appearances increasing. As far as the material realm is concerned, man has now all the possibilities of control. It is in the control of his emotions and of his passions that he is failing, so that finally the confrontation of the crisis of man can but lead to the spirit, to its condition and potential fate. Will man survive? Certainly not if he is to rely on the power he has found over the material realm alone; a progressive dehumanization and final annihilation is certain. Man can only survive in human terms, and that must mean a humanization of the environment. One knows that this is essentially a problem of emotionalizing this environment, and art could here and now give explicit directions as to how that should be done. The promise of an earthly paradise is there, within man's grasp.

But the question of timing and co-ordination comes into the picture: man must humanize his environment but he can only be equipped for doing so if he is in the first place truly a human being, if his humanizing drives are adequate to the task. It seems that something is missing.

One cannot help seeing in other ages, in other cultures, that whenever man rose to his greatest heights both in material achievement and in the achievements of art, he was fired by some underlying faith, some all-permeating creative power. Some sort of religious awareness is imperative, a basic, all-embracing attitude to life. As already emphasized, this should not be in some new revival, some new church; it needs no formulation at all. What is required perhaps pressingly is a realization that just as art is natural to man, and has, in fact, a biological explanation, so religion is a natural function, a function that belongs to the moiety of the human being beyond analysis, beyond description, and beyond formulation. The revolution of the new age should make such a relatively simple confrontation possible. Man is a state of feeling, not of what he believes himself to be. And religion is almost entirely there as soon as man is aware of the truth and necessity of it.

A miracle can be defined as an event which is not explicable by what is known or knowable. A work of art has this element of miracle about it: only a few ounces of material, and yet it can open up an endless universe of quite strange experience.

It is obvious that a thing is only miraculous to reason, the proof of reason's limitation. To an all-knowing agent, the term would be meaningless. The best that the human can sense is that the miracle is a part of nature, as did Ouspensky. One virtue of art is that it does make this miraculous quality apparent in all things also. In a sense, all is miracle, and the quality of it is only lost in the hustle and distractions of life. Art can bring it before one suddenly and forcefully.

The religious experience has also this about it, but instead of being paroxysmal and fragmentary as it is in art, the sensation of it becomes more enduring, the constant accompanying sense of the miracle of the human person, of the moment of living and being alive, of all creation.

CONCLUSION

IT is a commonly held notion that the painter's one and only business is to paint, implying that any other activity is misplaced and deleterious to his art. An intellectual approach to art is bound to be fatal, but it is possible to separate the two, the intellectual and the emotional. No painter can paint continually, and to indulge in a quite contrary activity for a while, which is what intellectual interests provide, can be beneficial rather than harmful.

Today, when so few people are concerned in the linking of art and life, in its most vital, valid forms, and so much that is being put over as an attempt at relationship is only concerned with the obsolete and the obsolescent, the artist is obliged to look around for himself. He is not the best placed person to do this: his approach is emotionally biased. But it has to be done, for no artist can work for a lifetime and fully unless he knows that his work is related to life, to society, to others. Whether his work is accepted or not is another matter. People can ignore him as long as he knows that the fault is theirs, not his.

Furthermore, this looking around is a source of enrichment. Even the most abstract art requires feed-in, and in some way, the diversified stimuli of modern life do get digested and do feed the emotional fires which in turn produce art. If one separates oneself from this pulsating life, then one's art invariably smoulders down. For the artist today modern life is fantastically rich in stimulation, in the way people live, work and feel and think, in the achievements of industry, of technology, in the miracles going on in laboratories and workshops, in the rocket-launching sites, in the deep tunnels and mines. Man becomes one vast feeling, exploring animal with countless antennae to feeling, and in some way, all this goes into art, even in its most synthetic forms, encoded, transformed as it would be in any computer.

And if the artist needs to be concerned at the human level, at the living, struggling, feeling level of others that make up his community and his world, he also must share in the magnificent adventure of the mind which is making man what he is, and what he can even now become, a god on earth; these have potent aspects to feeling, and are by no means purely intellectual. It is true today that an artist who despises the world as it is, who ignores the gropings of the human mind, in science, in industry, in the rivalries and clashes of opposing views, cannot be truly contemporary and cannot fully serve his age.

This book has been written with considerable difficulty, not only to indicate that art has a most important part to play in modern life, even in the survival of man, and that art has something to teach in all human views today, but also that it should serve as a stimulus to a review of the status and role of the artist in modern society.

The Bohemian heritage dies hard; to many, the artist is still a temperamental person, quite useless in all practical fields, and having no contribution to make to society. It is a pathetic view, and the artist is himself much to blame for it. If society gave the first slap, the artist retired into a pseudo-world of sulk and contempt, hating society and loathing science. In his own defence, he became a kind of hypersensitive moron, attempting a self-sufficiency in art which is impossible. The romantic artist moron persists, often encouraged by orthodox circles, by art schools as much as by critics. But there have been changes in art, and a new type of artist is emerging. It is now up to society to give him his chance.

If society has a higher regard for the worth and possible contribution of the artist, the artist would respond, just as we are usually funny when we are expected to be funny. In the Renaissance, the artist was often a godlike figure, a truly great, whole human being. Society has need of such people again, desperately, and it is up to society to bring them into being.

All too often the artist is sadly unequipped for the task to which he could be called. He is trivial and cynical. There is need for a world-wide conspiracy among artists themselves. The scientists and the technicians are taking over the world. It is up to artists and all the lovers of art to clamour for their place and influence in all those world-making and Universe-exploring drives of the modern age, the only assurance that the collapse of nature shall be succeeded by a man-made environment capable of fulfilling all truly human needs, the only guarantee that human beings shall at last become truly human. 'We are the transmuters of the earth' wrote Rilke, 'our whole existence here, the flights and falls of our love, all strengthen us for this task besides which there is really no other'.

NOTES

[1] Sir Russell Brain, *The Nature of Experience*, London, 1959; E. W. Tomlin, *Living and Knowing*, London, 1955.

[2] Charles Darwin, *The Expression of the Emotions in Man and Animals*, London, 1872.

[3] Desmond Morris, *The Biology of Art*, London, 1962. In a television interview, Dr. Morris emphasized the difference between the aesthetic function in man and in the ape by first stretching out his arms and then closing his fingers together. It is the evolution of emotionalism that separated man from the other anthropoids.

[4] A vast subject that still runs counter to popular views and behavioural requirements. G. Elliot Smith, *Human History*, London, 1934; H. S. Jennings, *The Biological Basis of Human Nature*, London, 1930; F. Alverdes. *Social Life in the Animal World*, London, 1927; B. Malinowski, 'Marriage', *Encyclopedia Britannica*, 14th edn.; Clellan S. Ford, *A Comparative Study of Human Reproduction*, London, 1945; James N. Spuhler, *The Evolution of Man's Capacity for Culture*, Detroit, 1959.

The provision of the hymen, which does not occur in other animals, would appear to be a morphological support for the psychological necessity of avoiding too early sex union, as well as for the avoidance of promiscuity prior to pairing. The removal of sex motivation from a hormonal cortical control makes possible the social enforcement of a biological necessity. See Marshall D. Sahlins, 'Origin of Society', *Scientific American*, 203 : 48, pp. 76–87, September, 1960. The relatively very poor immunity of human beings to the venereal diseases points to a relatively 'recent' origin of such diseases and a concomitant promiscuity, probably no farther back than the last ice age.

[5] The 'existential' emotions become parried by special devices; for instance, excitement passes into exhilaration, simple rhythms into complex and variable rhythms, awe into wonder, etc.

[6] Freud, in the wake of Nietzsche and the 'angry philosophers', takes it for granted that human nature is naturally evil, a Judeo-Christian bias, and so his humanizing drives can only arise somewhat artificially in society, a prodigious scientific myth. By assuming that the primitive subconscious is normally quiescent, like all discarded functions, and that it only becomes whipped up by abnormal stimuli, Freud's theories can be reinterpreted in a more humanly meaningful manner, and society acquires its far more creditable role of enforcing a natural function that is already there. With this in mind, all his works are worth the reading.

[7] Essence can be interpreted as the genetic, existential as the adaptation of essence to existence. In an unnatural, thwarting environment, it is necessarily the existential that predominates.

[8] An oscillative cosmology was always entertained in the East; S. Radhakrishnan, *History of Philosophy Eastern and Western*, London, 1952. It came through into Europe with Schopenhauer, Hegel, and Marx. See Fred Hoyle, *Frontiers of Astronomy*, London, 1955.

[9] Paleolithic cave art is a relatively recent art; the oldest human arts, made with perishable things such as flowers, are probably half a million years old. F. Avray Wilson, *Art into Life*, London, 1958.

[10] In some sensational fiction of the nineteenth and twentieth centuries, the jungle was looked on with euphoric eyes as the 'earthly paradise'—one sees something of this in Breughel. Anyone who has been into a tropical jungle will know that it is a green hell and its peoples harassed and mostly miserable.

[11] Brewster Ghiselin, *The Creative Process*, Berkeley (Cal.), 1952: 'For the creative order, which is an extension of life, is not an elaboration of the established, but a movement beyond . . .'

[12] Sir Herbert Read, *Art and Society*, London, 1937.

[13] The role of art is curiously neglected by Père Teilhard de Chardin.

[14] In a state of nature, nature reflects man, man nature—'Nature I loved, and next to nature, art' (Walter Savage Landor). To the extent that man can now humanize the environment he has made, he can humanize himself, and restore a broken bond with his environment.

[15] Henri Focillon, *L'An Mil*, Paris, 1952.

[16] Printed with a capital initial, Impressionism stands for the movement; with a small one, for the technical means and the appeals of naturalism made evident by the Impressionists.

[17] Repeated attempts, as by Biederman, and many recent exhibition introductions, to get out of the impasse of classicism in the geometric image, are all intellectual, not aesthetic.

[18] Classicism is the recurrent belief that order, established by precedent, is the only guide through contemporary uncertainties. T. S. Eliot: 'The important critic is the person who is absorbed in the present problems of art and who wishes to bring the forces of the past to bear on the solution of these problems' (*The Sacred Wood*, 1920). Classicism can be evident in the scientific mind, as it is in Sir D'Arcy Wentworth Thompson's *On Growth and Form*, London, 1942.

[19] J. J. Saunders, *The Age of Revolution*, London (1947); Raymond Williams, *Culture and Society*, London, 1959.

[20] Automation only exploits possibilities inherent in early industrialism; it brings in nothing new. The real break comes with atomic energy.

[21] Heinz Gartmann, *Science as History*, trans. A. G. Readett, London, 1960.

[22] Samuel C. Curran, *The Next Fifty Years*, London, 1962.

[23] M. Capek, *The Philosophical Aspect of Contemporary Physics*, Princeton, 1961.

[24] E. Cassirer *The Philosophy of Symbolic Forms*, trans. Ralph Manheim, London, 1953; A. N. Whitehead, *Symbolism: its Meaning and Effects*, London, 1928.

[25] A. N. Whitehead, *Science and the Modern World*, London, 1926.

[26] Anton Ehrenzweig, *The Psycho-Analysis of Artistic Vision and Hearing*, London, 1953.

[27] Joseph H. Woodger, *Biological Principles*, London, 1929.

[28] 'I believe it would be possible to trace changes in the climate of society and thought which made this particular discovery (non-Euclidean geometry) occur at that time and at no other. That is what I should call the large-scale correlation.' (C. P. Snow.)

'The writer of genius cannot help responding to the innermost needs of the age. . . . He cannot help becoming, through his own relation to his unconscious . . . an instrument of whatever there is in the general deep unconscious, its inner world of the whole age.' (J. B. Priestley, *Literature and Western Man*, London, 1960.)

[29] W. B. Bonnor, 'Einstein and the Nature of Space', *The Listener*, 26 March 1959. Eddington also hoped to find such a unitary principle. Attempts to find some unitarian exit out of quantum physics are periodical.

[30] I. A. Richards, 'Poetry as an Instrument of Research', *The Listener*, 17 September, 1959.

[31] Lancelot Law Whyte, *Aspects of Form*, London [1951]. Although organic forms tend to settle down into symmetry whenever they are allowed to do so, active new creation and new types depend on the asymmetries which persist in isolated conditions.

[32] Nagel, Ernest, and Newman, James R., *Gödel's Proof*, London, 1960.

[33] George Melhuish, *The Paradoxical Universe*, Bristol [1959].

[34] Norbert Wiener, *Cybernetics*, New York [1948]; Philip McCord Morse, *Methods of Operations Research*, Cambridge (Mass.) and New York, 1958.

[35] Eric Ashby and John Madge, *Athene*, vol. 9, no. 4.

[36] W. H. McCrea, *Nature*, 4730 : 1035, 1960.

[37] Joseph Needham, *Order and Life*, London, 1936.

[38] S. Giedion, *Mechanization Takes Command*, New York, 1948.

[39] F. A. Hayek, *The Counter-Revolution of Science*, Glencoe, Ill. [1952]; Herbert Feigl and M. Scriven (ed.), *The Foundations of Science and the Concepts of Psychology and Psycho-Analysis*, Minneapolis, 1956.

[40] Jean-Paul Sartre, *The Psychology of Imagination*, New York and

London, 1950; R. Klibansky (ed.), *Philosophy in the Mid-Century*, Florence, 1958.

[41] Dirac, see James Jeans, *The Growth of Physical Science*, London, 1947.

[42] Rosalind Heywood, *The Sixth Sense*, London, 1959.

[43] J. B. Rhine, *New Frontiers of the Mind*, London, 1937; H. J. Eysenck, *Sense and Nonsense in Psychology*, Harmondsworth, 1957.

[44] C. G. Jung and W. Pauli, *The Interpretation of Nature and the Psyche*, London, 1955; *The Times Literary Supplement*, 9 December, 1956.

[45] Henri Focillon, *see* review in *The Life of Forms in Art*, trans. C. B. Hogan and George Kubler, New Haven, 1942; Wilhelm Worringer, *Abstraction and Empathy*, trans. Michael Bullock, London, 1953. Although these authors attempt to treat their ideas as reasonably as possible, quite new concepts are suggested.

[46] Harold J. Blackham, *Six Existentialist Thinkers*, London, 1952 [1951].

[47] *Philosophy in the Mid-Century*, op. cit. in note 40 supra.

[48] Henry Burrows Acton, *The Illusion of the Epoch*, Boston, Mass., 1953.

[49] Karl R. Popper, *The Poverty of Historicism*, London, 1957.

[50] J. von Neumann and O. Morgenstern, *Theory of Games and Economic Behaviour*, Princeton, 1944; Richard Bevan Braithwaite, *The Theory of Games as a Tool for the Moral Philosopher*, London, 1955.

[51] Erich Fromm, *The Forgotten Language,* London, 1952; Philip E. Wheelwright, *The Burning Fountain: A Study in the Language of Symbolism*, Bloomington (Ind.), 1954; the 'depth' language of art as opposed to the 'steno' language of science.

[52] M. Weitz, 'Aesthetics in English-Speaking Countries', in *Philosophy in the Mid-Century*, op. cit. in note 40 supra.

[53] Maurice Bowra, *The Romantic Imagination*, London, 1950.

[54] 'I see the future, I plan the Universe, save mankind, I am utterly and completely immortal. I am even male and female.'

Custance, quoted in R. C. Zachner 'Mysticism. Sacred and Profane', London 1957.

See also section on the Samkhya philosophy in S. Radhakrishnan, *Indian Philosophy*, 2nd edn., London, 1929–31, vol. 2.

[55] Although Kinsey gives no hint of it, an increasing proportion of women would probably be found to reach orgasm today. In the last century only a small proportion did so; the orgasm was a male prerogative.

[56] C. G. Jung, *Psychology and Alchemy*, London, 1953; Mircea Eliade, *Forgerons et alchimistes*, Paris, 1950.

[57] Lewis Mumford, *The City in History*, New York, 1961.

[58] Sir Herbert Read, *A Concise History of Modern Painting*, London, 1959.

[59] G. Mathieu, *De l'abstrait au possible*, Paris, Cercle d'Art Contemporain, 1960.

[60] Colour-sensations can be produced by black and white contrasts. E. H. Land, 'Experiments in Color Vision', *Scientific American*, May 1959; W. Grey Walter, *The Living Brain*, London, 1953. Black and white vision preceded colour vision. See H. T. Pledge, *Science since 1500*, London, 1947. Red and yellow are the 'oldest' colours; blue, violet green sensitivity came specifically with humanization. Goethe found that red united all colours, as did Kandinsky; by transcendence, red, the most primitive colour, becomes the most spiritual.

[61] Quoted in Lancelot Law Whyte, *Aspects of Form*, London [1951].

[62] Herta Wescher, 'De Stael', *Cimaise*, April 1956.

[63] Hubert Benoit, *The Supreme Doctrine*, trans. Terence Gray, London, 1955; E. Herrigel, *Zen in the Art of Archery*, trans. R. F. C. Hull, London, 1953; Edward Conze, *Buddhist Meditation*, London, 1956; T. Christmas Humphreys, *Buddhism*, Harmondsworth, 1951. Zen is not easy to the European, yet every artist should make some attempt to come to some understanding of it. Nothing is ever viewed in the same way afterwards.

[64] Aldous Huxley, *The Doors of Perception*, London, 1954. The fact that such drugs as mescalin induce a 'naturalistic' type of pseudo-aesthetic emotion may go to explain why they are frequently felt to be unpleasant; either one enjoys them (and therefore indulges in the guilty relish of escapism), or if one is adapted to life as it is, one resists them fiercely. Laszlo Moholy-Nagy, *Vision in Motion*, Chicago, 1947.

[65] Evelyn Underhill, *Mysticism*, London, 1949.

[66] Rudolf Arnheim, *Art and Visual Perception*, London, 1956.

[67] J. C. Flugel, *Man, Morals, and Society*, London, 1945.

[68] Sir Herbert Read, *The Grass Roots of Art*, London, 1955; idem, *The philosophy of Modern Art*, London, 1952; idem, *Art and Society*, London, 1937; idem, *Art and Industry*, London, 1934.

[69] Gerald Reitling, *The Economics of Taste*, London, 1961.

[70] R. Alley, *Museums Journal*, June 1961.

[71] Full-page colour plate in *Encyclopedia Britannica*, 14th edn.

[72] Louis Sullivan's historic statement that form follows function should be corrected to 'form follows function which follows dynamic organisation'.

[73] T. Holzbog, 'A Situationist Architecture', *Fulbright Paris Review*, 1961.

[74] Margaret Mead, *Coming of Age in Samoa*, London, 1929; idem, *Sex and Temperament in Three Primitive Societies*, London, 1935.

[75] Abraham A. Moles, *Les Musiques experimentales*, Paris, 1960; L. A. Hiller, 'Computer music', *Scientific American*, December, 1959.

[76] *The Times*, 11 February 1962, for an account of work by Svoboda and others in Czechoslovakia.

[77] R. Gilman, 'Total Revolution in the Novel', *Horizon* (U.S.A.), 1962.

[78] Sir Herbert Read, *Education Through Art*, London, 1943.

[79] Sir Charles Snow, *The Two Cultures and the Scientific Revolution*, London, 1959, and review by Sir Eric Ashby, *Scientific American*, October 1959.

[80] J. Christopher Jones, *Athene*, 9 April 1961. Such attempts to rationalize art education quite ignore the essentially free, non-deterministic aspects of art, and are continuing attempts to spread out deterministic methods into non-deterministic fields. It would appear to be the case that the person who naturally tends to take up teaching as a vocation is prone to an orderly-mindedness that automatically favours a classical, geometric, pragmatic and essentially materialistic approach to the problems of communication, and to dissociative, analytical and compartmentalizing attitudes, evident in the Bauhaus, in its American and German succession today. The results are a very neat, functional, catalogued product and aesthetics and for this reason more effectively teachable, but an essential aspect of contemporary feeling is unfortunately omitted.

[81] 'I have forced myself to contradict myself in order to avoid conforming to my own taste.' (Marcel Duchamp.)

[82] Man as an open, unfinished incomplete challenge. L. Eiseley, 'An Evolutionist looks at Modern Man', in Richard Thruelsen and John Kober (eds.), *Adventures of the Mind*, London, 1960. Wiener sees every living organism as an 'open system'. Lewis Mumford: 'Freedom combats power.'

[83] 'Religion is the vision of something that stands beyond, behind, and within, the passing flux of immediate things; something which is real, and yet awaiting to be realized; something which is a remote possibility, and yet the greatest of present facts; something that gives meaning to all that passes, and yet eludes apprehension . . .' (A. N. Whitehead, *Science and the Modern World*, London, 1926.)

[84] The religious element in Marxism has been repeatedly noted; it is a continuation of the Judaeo-Christian optimism of man's eventual salvation. 'Marx professed himself an atheist, but retained a cosmic optimism which only theism could justify.' Bertrand Russell, *History of Western Philosophy*, London, 1946, p. 816.

[85] 'The psychic fact "God" is a typical autonomism, a collective archetype, as I later called it. It is therefore characteristic not only of all

higher forms of religion, but appears spontaneously in the dreams of individuals . . . it has a reality independent of the attitude of the conscious mind. It is a psychic existent which should not in itself be confused with the idea of a metaphysical God.' G. C. Jung, *Symbols of Transformation*, trans. R. F. C. Hull, London, 1956, p. 56n. See also R. Wilhelm and C. G. Jung, *The Secret of the Golden Flower*, London, 1932. The psychic reality of Jung is not consciously entertainable; if it does coincide with a metaphysical reality, then that reality cannot be known consciously. The conscious claim of God would rest on the same recurring infirmity of reason, common to the prevalent insistence on an exclusively rational universe. For an emergent idea of deity, see Samuel Alexander, *Space, Time, and Deity*, London, 1920.

[86] Julian Huxley (ed.), *The Humanist Frame*, London, 1961. It is difficult not to sense a certain indefinable mysticism in the writing, which makes it something more than merely rational.

[87] Gerald J. Whitrow, *The Natural Philosophy of Time*, London, 1961.

[88] *Man and Time: Papers from the Eranos Yearbooks*, 3, ed. Joseph Campbell, London, 1958; Etienne Souriau, 'Time in the Plastic Arts', in Susanne K. Langer (ed.), *Reflections on Art*, Baltimore, 1958.

[89] J. E. Cirlot, *A Dictionary of Symbols*, London, 1962.

[90] Malcolm E. de Chazal, *La Vie filtrée* [Paris], 1949.

GENERAL INDEX

For names of authors and artists see the Index of Names.

INDEX OF NAMES

Names of authors appearing in the Notes, and the names of artists accompanying the illustrations at the back of the book, are not included.

THE illustrations which follow refer to the main kinds of painting described in the text. Such groupings are perforce arbitrary, and the work of many painters overlaps into several groups. The lists of names opposite each illustration are of painters whose work happens to be known to the writer; serious omissions are inevitable.

Choice has been purely visual, and no account has been taken of the classifications of others. Critics can 'see' almost anything into a work of art, and artists often enough talk one way and paint another. English painters especially have a habit of looking for naturalistic references in their work, although their work does at times attain an apparent independence, which is what matters here.

ABSTRACT EXPRESSIONISM

Arnal
Avray Wilson
Baz
Bertini
Bowen
Bruning
Bryen
Coplans
Cordell
Crippa
Cuixart
Damian
Davie
De Kooning
Fidler
Francken
Franckenthaler
Fruhmann
Haller
Hantai
Hartung
Horrocks

Plate 1. Kirchberger
(Galerie Muller, Stuttgart).

Plate 2. Milnes Smith.

ABSTRACT EXPRESSIONISM (*Cont.*)

Hofmann
Kirchberger
Levee
Macsparran
Millares
Milnes Smith
Morita
Motherwell
Phaler
Pollock
Sonderborg
Spazzapan
Spiess
Stapleton
Tworkov
Vandercam
Vielfaure
Viola
Walker
Wendt
Wicht
Yunkers

Plate 3. Davie
(Gimpel Fils, London).

Plate 4. Avray Wilson.

CALLIGRAPHIC

Al Copley
Childs
Degottex
Fink
Hartung
Mathieu
Michaux
Nalecz
Sanfillipo
Soto
Stubbing
Tobey
Tomlin
Wynter

Plate 5. Al Copley (Drian Gallery, London)

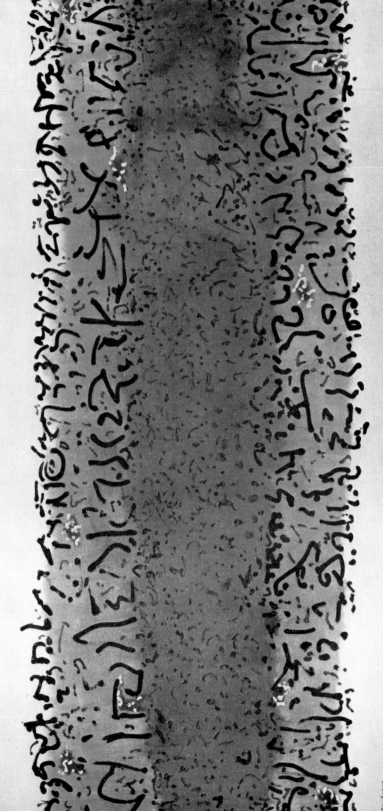

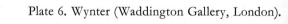

Plate 6. Wynter (Waddington Gallery, London).

SEMANTIC

Accardi
Capogrossi
Chryssa
Dorazio
Jurgen Fischer
Kusania
Lattanzi
Richenberg

Plate 7. Dorazio (New Vision Centre Gallery, London

KINETIC

Agam
Götz
Kosice
Mack
Schoeffer
Sonderborg
Takis
Tinguely
Yanagi

Plate 8. Agam (Drian Gallery, London).

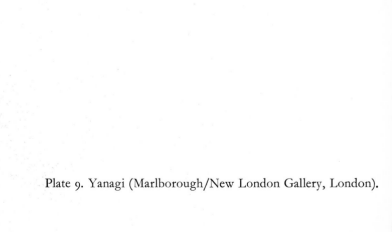

Plate 9. Yanagi (Marlborough/New London Gallery, London).

THE UNPAINTERLY

Blow
Benjamin
Davie
Frankenthaler
Hassel Smith
Hilton
Johnson
Leslie

Plate 10. Blow (Gimpel Fils, London

Plate 11. Hassel Smith (Richard Weil Es

FIELDS OF FORCE

Borduas
Frost
Guitet
Heath
Koenig
Louis
Phaler
Still

Plate 12. Phaler (Galerie Muller, Stuttga▪

MULTIPLE

Avray Wilson
Brion Gysin
Jensen
Richter
Rauschenberg

Plate 13. Avray Wils▪

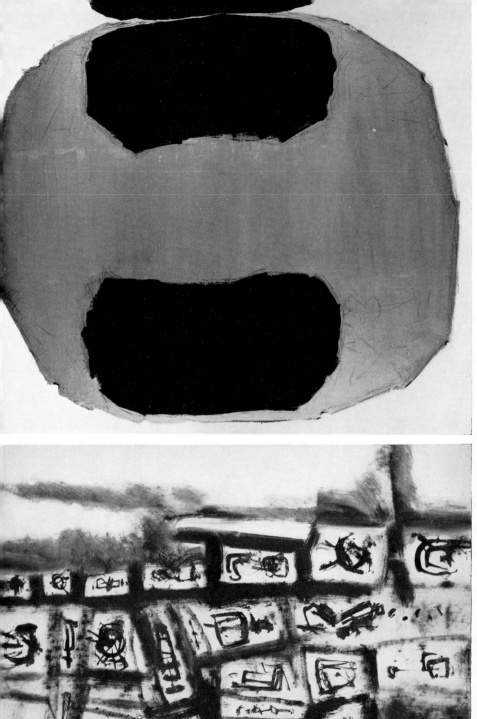

MYTH

Belcher
Burri
Crippa
Jasper Johns
Hassel Smith
Mc Hale
Rivers
Smith

NEO-DADA

Dove
Rotella
Rauschenberg

ASSEMBLAGE

Arman
Belcher
Cornell
Latham
Mallary
Tinguely
Wagemaker

Plate 14. Belcher (A.I.A. Gallery, London).

ABSTRACT SURREALISM

Bowen
Cannizzaro
Cooper
Crippa
Damian
Feito
Foldes
Fontana
Haller
Jenkins
Mara
Smith
William

Plate 15. Bowen.

Plate 16. Jenkins (Arthur Tooth, London).

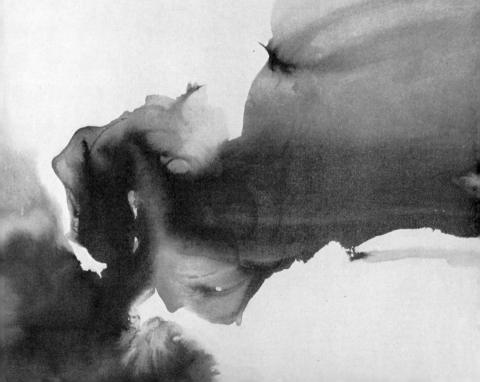

MATTER PAINTINGS

Aesbacher
Alley
Blow
Bogart
Burri
Chapman
Clemente
Coetzee
Crippa
Cuixart
Fautrier
Feito
Jadot
Kepes
Kerg
Klein
Krajcberg
Newcombe
Saito
Schumacher
Tapies
Wagemaker
Yoshishige

Plate 17. Bogart
(Gimpel Fils, London)

Plate 18. Aeschbacher (New Vision
Centre Gallery, London).

META IMAGE

Bill
Candappa
Farmer
Gottlieb
Heron
Klein
Louis
Mack
Newman
Noland
Rothko
Scott
Stabell
Stamos
Still

SOFT EDGE

Farmer
Newman
Samona
Stamos

Plate 19. Farmer (A.I.A. Gallery, London).

Plate 20. Samona (Molton Gallery, London).

SIMPLE

Barré
Bissier
Compard
Degottex
Keyser
Parker

Plate 21. Bissier (Gimpel Fils, London

ABSTRACT REALISM

Hassel Smith
Hultberg
Jasper Johns
Rivers

Plate 22. Rivers (Gimpel Fils, London